Asherah

American University Studies

Series VII
Theology and Religion
Vol. 74

PETER LANG
New York • Bern • Frankfurt am Main • Paris

Richard J. Pettey

Asherah

Goddess Of Israel

PETER LANG
New York • Bern • Frankfurt am Main • Paris

Library of Congress Cataloging-in-Publication Data

Pettey, Richard J.
Asherah : goddess of Israel / Richard J. Pettey.
p. cm. – (American university studies. Series VII, Theology and religion ; vol. 74)
Includes bibliographical references and index.
1. Asherah (Semitic deity) 2. Mythology, Canaanite. 3. Israel–Antiquities. 4. Palestine–Religious life and customs. I. Title. II. Series.
BL1605.A7P48 1990 299'.26–dc20 90-35025
ISBN 0-8204-1306-2 CIP
ISSN 0740-0446

Printed by Weihert-Druck GmbH, Darmstadt, West Germany

Table of Contents

List of Tables

Acknowledgments

Special thanks are due to Dr. Sharon Pace Jeansonne of the Theology Department of Marquette University and to my colleagues in the Milwaukee Old Testament Reading Group.

This book is dedicated to the women who have challenged me and supported me.

Asherah

Introduction

Baking under the Israeli sun in 1987, I and my fellow excavators were searching the ancient remains of the Philistine city of Ekron, located on the site of Tel Miqne, on the property of Kibbutz Revadim. I saw a crowd gathering a few yards away from me, straining to see an artifact. Numbed by the sheer volume of artifacts we had already uncovered, my colleagues would only have been attracted by something unusual. Dropping my tools, I went to see. It was a broken terra cotta plaque, about the size of my palm, bearing the image of a goddess. I knew right away who it was. "This is an Asherah," I exclaimed, excited beyond my wildest dreams and proud to be the first to identify her.

Indeed, recent archaeological discoveries have suggested that there was a Canaanite goddess who was not only worshiped by the people of ancient Israel during the time of the monarchy (around 1000 to 587 B.C.E), but who was so much associated with Yahweh as to be construed as Yahweh's consort. The inscriptions and artifacts which have raised this startling question suggest the need for a complete study of this goddess, Asherah.

Using a largely inductive approach, Parts I, II, and III of this book collect the information. Part I investigates the Canaanite and ancient near eastern backgrounds of Asherah, defining the goddess and her characteristics. Part II, the central element of this study, considers the biblical texts in which Asherah is found. Part III assembles the archaeological evidence for the existence of an Asherah cult, including the inscriptions and artifacts mentioned above. Part IV concludes the study with some observations about the question of Asherah as the goddess of Israel.

PART I

BACKGROUNDS

Who was this Asherah, where did she come from? Known by several names, mother goddess Asherah had roots in many of the cultures of the Ancient Near East. Her Canaanite origins, however, had the most significant influence on the Israelites, who were neighbors of the Canaanites. Especially in the literature of ancient Ugarit can one find information about the goddess whom the Hebrews and Israelites adopted. There one finds a mother goddess who was a central figure in the ancient cult, the consort of El, who would, after being adopted by the Israelites, become known as the consort of Yahweh.

Chapter 1

Asherah in Ancient Ugarit

Understanding a pantheon is not an easy task. Rarely does one god or goddess occupy a clearly defined position. A goddess such as Asherah had roles which changed over the decades. She can easily be confused with goddesses like Ishtar or Astarte, and in some instances should be, because her role and even her identity overlap with the others. The records are incomplete, implications are subtle, and the results of the research uncertain. Yet an attempt at understanding is necessary in order to increase one's knowledge of the Asherah whom Israel adopted from the Canaanites. This chapter is devoted to the Ugaritic literature, whose tablets remained undiscovered until 1929. They are the richest extra-biblical source for understanding Asherah.

The literature of Ugarit is not isolated from the history of world literature. Ugarit was a crossroads, a place of mercantile and cultural exchange. Its literature is rich with the influence of other peoples. Cyrus Gordon has hailed this literature as a teacher to both the Semites and the Indo-Europeans.[1] He argued that its literature anticipates both Hebrew and Greek literature, and its alphabet was used by both the Israelites and the Greeks.

There are three major epics in the Ugaritic literature, the Baal cycle, the epic of Keret, and the Aqhat epic. The last of these is of no concern for this study since its story and circumstances, which relate to the ancient sage Daniel of Ez 14:14, rarely mention Asherah. The other texts, which come from the Phoenician area and were copied between the 17th and 15th centuries B.C.E., present our only picture of a complete pantheon in any one period.[2] The Baal cycle contains the chief elements of the pantheon including lists of deities, the myths of their interaction, and information about their characters and roles. The epic of Keret is the escapades of a heroic king of Ugarit named Keret, whose religious practices provide some information about the deities.

The pantheon revealed in this literature is complex. Relationships are hopelessly fluid. Particular divine functions, such as those of Asherah, Astarte, Anat, or of El and Baal, are shared by several deities, and the deities seem to develop or even change as the story progresses. Moreover, as P. Miller suggested, the foreign influence on the composition of this pantheon was great, including Mesopotamian and West-Semitic sources.[3] These will become evident as this study progresses.

In the pantheon of Ugarit, Asherah is no more or less difficult to understand than any other major deity; that is to say, that after a great deal of attention, the results are not as rich as one might hope for. Yet the facts as presented in this study will present a clearer picture than has been heretofore available, an undetailed but distinct picture of a goddess important to the peoples of ancient Canaan.

1. The Name and Title of Asherah

"Asherah" is actually a hebraeicized form of the Ugaritic *ʾṯrt*, extant 62 times. It will be vocalized hereafter as 'Athirat.' Lest there be any question that Athirat and Asherah are one and the same, note that in the development of the Semitic languages the change from Ugaritic to Hebrew produced patterns which, among others, included the transformation of the early 'th' (*ṯ*) sound to the later 'sh' sound. This is well attested by Cross and others.[4] Thus the 'th' in Athirat became the 'sh' in Asherah. The vocalization differences are of little concern in these consonantal languages, especially regarding the root origins of the words. The final 'h' in Asherah replaces the 't' and can be interpreted simply as the Hebrew feminine singular suffix, which is the expected Hebrew adaptation for the name of a female deity.

In a further development, Cross noted that in the Ugaritic language Athirat is not only a proper name, but also a verb form. He said that Athirat is "a perfect verb, formally stative, from the fuller name *athirat yammi*, 'she who treads upon the sea.[5] It is, therefore, apparent that in the Ugaritic culture this goddess was related to the sea. This is not surprising when one recalls that Ugarit was a mercantile center which, since it adjoins a major seaport, would have housed countless people related to the shipping trade, who doubtless would have been loyal to a sea deity of some kind. She was Athirat, their protectress in the sea, protecting them from the watery chaos.

2. The Baal Cycle

By far the most complete study of Athirat in the Ugaritic literature was done by Alice L. Perlman.[6] While a full-scale treatment of the texts would be largely a repetition of her work, for the sake of completeness a few of the key texts should be re-examined for the purpose of clarifying the identity of Athirat.

The first two texts come from the Baal cycle. First is a text segment in which the story finds Baal, Anat, and several others approaching Athirat. The approach of this powerful contingent frightened her, but the sight of a huge throne of gold and silver which had earlier been given her by a craftsman-god restored her confidence. She then continued with her work of directing her fisherman. Thereafter, she was astonished to find the contingent paying homage to her.

II AB ii 12-36[7]

12 bnšỉ.^{e}nh.wtphn	Lifting her eyes, Athirat perceived,
13 hlk̉ b^{e}l.ảŧtrt (14) kt^{e}n.	she surely sighted the coming of Baal,
hlk.btlt (15)^{e}nt[.]	the coming of the virgin Anat,

	tdrq.ybmt (16) [lỉmm].	the speedy approach of the sister-in-law [of peoples].
	bh.p^{e}nm (17) [tṭṭ.]	At that (her) feet [stamped], [she burst]
	[b^{e}]dn.ksl (18) [tŧbr.]	(her) loins [round] about,
	[^{e}ln.p]np.td[^{e}]	her face sweated [above],
19	tǵṣ[.pnt.ks]lh	she convulsed [the joints of] her loins,
20	ảns.de.ẓr[h]	the muscles of [her] back.
21	tšủ.gh.wtṣḥ[.]	She lifted up her voice and cried:
	[ỉ]k (22) mǵy.ảlỉyn[.b]^{e}l	'How (is it that) mightiest Baal has arrived?
23	ỉk.mǵyt.b[t]lt (24) ^{e}nt	'How (is it that) the virgin Anat has arrived?
	mḫṣy hm[.m]ḫṣ (25) bny.	'Are my enemies come to smite my sons
	hm[.mkly.ṣ]brt (26) ảryy[.]	'or [make an end of] the company of my kinsfolk?'
	[ẓl].ksp.[a]trt (27) kt^{e}n.	(But) when Athirat sighted [the coverings] of silver,
	zl. ksp.wn[b]t (28) ḫrṣ.	(when she sighted) the coverings of silver and coatings of gold,
	šmh.rbt.ả[ŧrt] (29) ym.	dame Athirat of the sea did rejoice.

	gm.lǵlmh,k[tṣḥ]	Surely [she cried] aloud to her page:
30	^{e}n.mkŧr.åp t[---]	'Look on the craftsmanship, even [ ]
31	dgy.rbt.åŧr[t.ym]	'[o] fisherman of dame Athirat [of the sea].
32	qh.rŧt.bdk.q[dš]	'Take a net in your hand, [Qodesh],
33	rbt.^{e}l.ydm[.åmrr]	'a large one on (your) two hands, [Amrur];
34	bmdd.ỉl,y[m----]	'into Yam, the darling of El [ ]
35	bym.ỉl.d[----bn]	'into Yam, the god of [ ]
36	hr.ỉl.y[-------]	'[into] Nahar, the god of [ ]

Verses 14-15 shed light on the identity of Athirat and Anat. Because of their meeting face to face, it can be concluded that, at least in this epic, Athirat and Anat are clearly distinguished, one from the other, and do not overlap in their identities.

Athirat displays fear when, in verses 16 and following, Anat and Baal enter. This reveals the power of Anat and Baal, such that even Athirat, the chief goddess and consort of El, shivers and quakes for fear that they might harm her family, which is the family of most of the deities of this pantheon. However, it is also noteworthy that Anat and Baal came not to frighten Athirat, but rather to beg for her help, asking her to intercede for them to El for permission to construct a palace for Baal. Even though Athirat feared them she nevertheless ranked above them and wielded power and influence over them. Thus it is apparent that a vital tension of power existed in this top level of the deities.

Athirat's questions in verses 22-26 show that she was in no way omniscient. Athirat needed to ask in order to obtain information regarding the mission of Anat and Baal. Also apparent in her question is that Baal is not among those deities who are her sons. How is it that Athirat is the mother of all the deities, (though not El, her consort, naturally) except Baal?[8] Baal is the son of El, but Athirat is not his mother as she is of all the rest.[9] This is rather untidy, a sign that perhaps the pantheon has been tampered with over the generations, and may indicate that deities from elsewhere have entered this pantheon and taken a place among the rest, but whose relationships with other deities have not been totally enmeshed in the system of the pantheon. Athirat is certainly a candidate for this status. Within this narrative she is called mother of all the deities except Baal. Yet Baal is second in command to the chief God, El, above all Athirat's children. Perhaps the ancient epic is saying that Athirat is welcome, but cannot be allowed to be construed as prior to El's first born, Baal. The tension of power could be rooted in the fact that Athirat entered the pantheon after Baal and assumed the position of El's consort, thus creating a rivalry for power between herself and El's first-born.

When, in verses 26-28, Athirat catches sight of her throne of silver and gold, she remembers her position, that she is the esteemed consort of El and the progenetrix of all the other deities. This thought consoles her and allays her fear of Baal and Anat. Alone she might have reasons to fear, but in alliance with El and her divine children she is safe. This fact supports the theory that Athirat might be the newcomer into the pantheon. On her own merits Athirat does not hold power, but as welcomed by El and as mother of his children, she has gained a protected position of power.

Verse 28 reveals Athirat's title. Here we have her official title, Lady Athirat of the Sea, *Athirat Yammi*.

After her fright has subsided, in verses 28-35 Athirat goes back to her business. What was she doing? She was guiding the work of seafarers, in this case the fishing trade. Note that the sea itself is referred to as El's beloved, or darling. It is no wonder that his beloved goddess has the honor of tending this beloved part of his kingdom, the sea.

II AB iii 23-35[10]

23	ảḫr.mǵy.ảliỷn.b^{e}l	Afterwards mightiest Baal did arrive
24	mǵyt.btlt.^{e}nt	(and) the Virgin Anat did arrive;
25	tmgnn.rbt[.a]ṯrt ym	they importuned dame Athirat of the sea,
26	tǵẓyn.qnyt ỉlm	entreated the creatress of the gods.
27	wt^{e}n.rbt.ảṯrt ym	And dame Athirat of the sea answered:
28	ỉk tmgnn.rbt (29) ảṯrt.ym	'How should you importune dame Athirat of the sea,
	tǵẓyn (30) qnyt.ỉlm.	entreat the creatress of the gods?
	mgntm (31) ṯr.ỉl.dpỉd.	Have you importuned the bull, kindly god,
	hm.ǵẓtm (32) bny.bnwt	or entreated the creator of creatress?'
	wt^{e}n (33) btlt.^{e}nt.	And the virgin Anat answered:
	nmgn (34) [ủ]m.rbt.ảṯrt.ym	'we will importune (our mother dame Athirat of the sea,
35	[nǵ]ẓ.qnyt.ỉlm	'[we] will entreat the creatress of the gods.

In verses 25 and following, Anat and Baal do homage to Athirat. Is this homage sincere or mocking? In either case, it has a motive: to enlist Athirat's help in interceding before El on behalf of Baal's need to gain permission to have a palace built for himself.

Mention is made in verse 26 of Athirat's role as progenitress of the gods, a reminder that she is the consort of El.

The image of El used in Canaanite literature is the bull. El is the creator, as the image in verse 31 suggests.

3. The Epic of Keret

Keret A iv 197-206[11]

197	ym[ǵy.]lqdš (198) ả[ṯrt.]ṣrm.	He came to the sanctuary of Athirat of the two Tyres
	wlỉlt (199) ṣd[ny]m.	and to (the sanctuary of) Elat of the Sidonians.
	ṯm (200) ydr[.k]rt.ṯ^{e}	There the noble Keret vowed, (saying):
201	ỉ ỉṯṯ.ảṯrt.ṣrm	'As surely as Athirat of the two Tyres
202	wỉlt.ṣdynm	'and Elat of the Sidonians exists,
203	hm.ḥry.bty. (204) ỉqḥ.	'if I may take Huray (into) my house,
	ǎš^{e}rb.ǵlmt (205) ḥẓry.	'introduce the lass to my court,
	ṯnh.wspm (206) ảtn.	'I will give twice her (weight) in silver
	w.ṯlṯn.ḫrṣm	'and thrice her (weight) in gold.'

King Keret deeply desired to make the maiden Huray his bride. In order to insure the success of his journey to find her, he stopped in Phoenicia and invoked the help of Athirat, making a vow to her on the condition that Huray becomes his wife.

In verse 197, mention is made of a sanctuary of Athirat, a place of presence and worship, implying that Athirat was not only an epic character, but that Athirat was also a deity of note among the Canaanites, a deity who was worshiped in her sanctuary. Gibson noted that the two Tyres are the two geographical areas of one Tyre, the island and the mainland.[12]

Athirat was a goddess not only in Tyre, but also in Sidon, according to verses 198-199 of the epic. This seems quite appropriate since Athirat is the goddess of the sea, and both cities were major seaports and shipping centers. 'Elat' is the feminine form of 'el' and means 'goddess' in a rather general way, just as 'el' means 'god.' However in this text it is clear that 'elat' is applied to Athirat as a title, nearly a name, just as the chief 'el' is called 'El.' This implies her high stature in the pantheon. Whereas there are other goddesses in the pantheon, the only one called 'Elath' is Athirat.

Keret's acknowledgment of Athirat and his vow to give a substantial gift of silver and gold in return for his marriage to Huray (verses 200-207) has a number of implications regarding the people who composed the epic. 1) They believed that Athirat was a living deity, not merely a relic. 2) Athirat was a goddess of note, having the power to grant such favors as Keret requested. 3) Athirat's power is seen here in a non-aquatic setting. Hence her sphere of influence and power was seen to extend beyond the bounds of the sea and sea-related matters such as fishing and sailing. It would seem natural, in any case, that a goddess with the power and rank of Asherah would not be limited to the sea. One would expect her to have influence in the affairs which take place on land. 4) Athirat could be either appeased or influenced by material gifts such as gold and silver. 5) There was a sanctuary of Athirat where these gifts could be presented by those who sought her favors. 6) Since such a gift-receiving sanctuary existed, it must have been necessary to have at least a minimum of sanctuary officials who could receive such gifts and do with them whatever was appropriate. The implication here is that there was some kind of cult organized around the goddess Athirat.[13]

Keret B ii 21-28[14]

21	ả[ŧt.tq]ḥ.ykrt.	'the [wife whom you]take, O Keret,
	ảŧt (22) tqḥ.btk.	'the wife whom you take (into) your house,

	g̔lmt.tš^{e}rb (23) ḥqrk.	'the lass whom you introduce to your court,
	tld.šb^{e}.bnm.lk	'shall bear you seven sons,
24	wŧmn tŧtmnm (25) lk	'and get you indeed eight;
	tld.yṣb.g̔lm	'she shall bear the lad Yassib,
26	ynq.ḥlb.a̓[ŧ]rt	'one that shall suck the milk of Athirat
27	mṣṣ.ŧd.btlt.[^{e}nt]	'one that shall drain the breasts of the virgin [Anat],
28	mšnq[t. ı̓lm---]	'the suckling nurses of [the gods].'

El promised that Huray would bear eight sons of King Keret. One of these sons was to be singled out and treated in a special way. This son, Yassib, was to be suckled by Athirat and Anat themselves.[15]

G. W. Ahlström saw a relationship between Huray and Athirat. Huray is Keret's queen and Athirat is the queen of heaven, the queen of El the sky god. They share the duties of mothering Yasab, the heir of Keret. Noting that in Keret A iii 147-149 Huray is described in terms appropriate to a statue of a goddess, he says:

> There is thus an intimate connection between the queen and the virgin goddess, a connection reflected in the fact that when the virgin goddess has given birth to the divine child she can be called 'mother-goddess' and when the queen, after the *hieros gamos*, has given birth to the future king and has seen her son's enthronement, she becomes 'queen mother' and virtually the *paredros* of the king. Her position is an earthly replica of that of the mother of the god.[16]

One might note that in verses 26 and 27 the goddesses Athirat and Anat appear as equal parties in a parallel construction. One might then argue from this text that they are the same goddess. This argument does not stand up under the scrutiny of comparison with the same deities in the Baal cycle, who are portrayed in that context as indisputably distinct. Furthermore, this comparison is not made elsewhere in the Keret epic. A possible explanation for the juxtaposition of these goddesses in this text comes from observation of another text in the Keret epic.[17] This text shows Anat in parallel not with Athirat, but with Astarte. The confusion among these three deities is apparent. The epic writers saw similarities among these deities, as in the Keret epic, which was dominated by Asherah, but whose role was occasionally asociated with both Anat and Astarte.

4. The Epic of Shachar and Shalim

It is without doubt that Athirat can be called the goddess of the sea and the coastal areas. It is noteworthy, however, that even in these early epics her identity as a desert goddess or inland goddess is foreshadowed. She is described as having given birth to the gods in the desert areas,[18] and is described in II AB iv-v 14 as having ridden a donkey, an animal better suited for the steppes than the waves. One would expect that since the local economies embraced the land and its fruits, the influence of Athirat's protection would also be associated with inland affairs. It is in the inland sphere that the Israelites had their primary encounter with Athirat.

One final reference in the Ugaritic texts which supports the association of Athirat with inland territories is a set of two texts which connect Athirat with the field. It appears in the epic of *Shachar and Shalim and the Gracious Gods*.

SS 13 and 28[19]

13	wšd.šd ỉlm.	Then (shall be sung) 'The field(s), the field(s) of the gods,
	šd ảŧrt.wrḥm<y>.	'the field(s) of Athirat and Rahmay.'
28	šd<.šd>[ỉ]lm.	'The fields(s) <the field(s)> of the gods,
	šd.ảŧrt.wrḥmy	'the field(s) of Athirat and Rahmay,'

This text does little more than mention a connection between Atirat and the field which is not a usual part of her association in the

Ugaritic literature. One suspects that this association comes from a non-Ugaritic origin; that Athirat was probably a part of the pantheons of inland peoples at least as ancient as Ugarit. If such were the case, it would be likely that at least a few remnants of her characteristics would have migrated to Ugarit with her name. Such characteristics will be noted in the next chapter.

It is clear that Asherah is the linguistic equivalent of Athirat, the leading goddess of the Ugaritic pantheon. She was first the goddess of the sea, honored and hallowed by seafarers especially at Canaanite port cities, such as Tyre and Sidon.

The Baal cycle reveals Athirat as the highest ranking goddess in the Canaanite pantheon, and superior to all gods except the chief god, El, and Baal, to whom she is not related but with whom she is in contention for power. She is the mother of all the gods except El and Baal.

The Keret epic affirms her high stature in the pantheon and reveals that there was a cult of Athirat. Some of the worship of Athirat took place in sanctuaries. She had the power to grant favors and did so as the result of appeasements in the form of gifts of gold and silver. This presumes the presence of cultic personnel who received and disposed of such gifts in her name.

Another interesting feature of the Keret epic is the relationship of Athirat to the king of Ugarit. She appears, along with the king's wife, as the co-mother of the king's heir to the throne. She was said to suckle the young prince. Thus Athirat can be described as the divine guarantor of the throne, and the king can be described as the legitimate offspring of Athirat.

A minor Ugaritic piece, the epic of *Shachar and Shalim*, verifies that Athirat had a strong influence in the inland areas, not only on the sea. This point is of particular importance in making the connection between Athirat and the Israelites. The Israelites were not a sea people but were nomads and farmers. They had no reason to develop a liking for a sea goddess. But if Athirat/Asherah was also an inland goddess, then there is the possibility that they would have found her patronage desirable.

Notes

1 Cyrus H. Gordon, *Before the Bible: The Common Background of Greek and Hebrew Civilisations* (London: Collins, 1962), pp. 129-55.

2 James B. Pritchard, ed., *Ancient Near Eastern Texts Relating to the Old Testament*, 3rd ed. with sup. (New Jersey: Princeton University Press, 1969), p. 149; E. Theodore Mullen Jr., *The Divine Council in Canaanite and Early Hebrew Literature*, Harvard Semitic Monographs, no. 24 (Chico, Calif.: Scholars Press, 1980), p. 2; Helmer Ringgren, *Religions of the Ancient Near East*, trans. John Sturdy (Philadelphia: Westminster Press, 1973), pp. 140-53; William Foxwell Albright, *Yahweh and the Gods of Canaan: A Historical Analysis of Two Contrasting Faiths* (London: Athlone Press, 1968), p. 102; Walter Beyerlin, ed., *Near Eastern Religious Texts Relating to the Old Testament*, Old Testament Library (Philadelphia: Westminster Press, 1978), pp. 185-90. Texts are cited, unless otherwise noted, according to the sigla of their first modern editor, C. Virolleaud, published over a period of years (the 1930's and 1940's) in *Syria*.

3 Patrick D. Miller, Jr., "Ugarit and the History of Religions," *Journal of Northwest Semitic Languages* 9 (1981): 119-128.

4 Yohanan Aharoni, *The Land of the Bible: A Historical Geography*, trans. and ed. A. F. Rainey, enlarged ed. (Philadelphia: Westminster Press, 1979), p. 114 (chart); Frank Moore Cross, *Canaanite Myth and Hebrew Epic* (Cambridge: Harvard University Press, 1973), p. 53 (chart).

5 Cross, *Canaanite Myth*, p. 67.

6 Alice Lenore Perlman, *Asherah and Astarte in the Old Testament and Ugaritic Literatures*, a dissertation for the Graduate Theological Union, Berkeley, California (Ann Arbor: University Microfilms International, 1979), pp. 39-96. Perlman disagrees with Cross saying that Athirat is not a verbform but a proper name (pp.74-78).

7 J. C. L. Gibson, *Canaanite Myths and Legends*, 2nd ed. (Edinburgh: T. & T. Clark, 1978), pp. 56-7.

8 II AB i 20.

9 II AB iv-v 43.

10 Gibson, *Canaanite Myths*, p. 58.

11 Gibson, *Canaanite Myths*, pp. 87-8.

12 Gibson, *Canaanite Myths*, p.87.

13 Cf. William Foxwell Albright, "A Vow to Asherah in the Keret Epic," *Bulletin of the American Schools of Oriental Research* 94 (April 1944): 30-31. Albright would disagree with Gibson's rendering of ʾ*iṯ* as "exist." He says, "This word has hitherto remained unexplained; it is certainly (H. L. Ginsberg agrees) the feminine of ʾ*iṯ* 'he is (present).' The correctness of this simple solution is shown by the parallelism between ʾ*iṯ Bʿl* and *ḥy Bʿl*, which corresponds, of course, to the Hebrew *ḥay Yahweh*, 'as YHWH lives.' It is important linguistically to learn that Heb. *yēš* (also written ʾ*ēš*) is a stative form like *gēr*, probably from a stem ʾ*wṯ* or *ywṯ*. Semantically we must beware of rendering ʾ*iṯ* as 'exist'; like Heb. *yēš* it means 'be (concretely) present' (cf. its use with the name *Yahweh* in Gen. 28:16 and Jud. 6:13). This point is important in connection with the evaluation of O. T. theology, which is empirico-logical, not ontological." (p. 31, note 12) Thus the cultic implication is even stronger with Albright's translation, "Athirat of Tyre is present." D. Winton Thomas, ed., in *Documents from Old Testament Times* (New York: Harper, Torchbook, 1958) on p. 122 gives a variant position. He disagrees with the common translation of ʾ*athrt tsrm* as "Athirat of the Tyrians" and calls it "Athirat of deposits" from a cognate with the Arabic *tsurra*, "a bundle." He also calls ʿ*elt tsdynm* "the goddess of oracles" after the Arabic cognate *tsaday*, "re-echo."

I think Thomas has said too much. Albright's simpler explanation makes more sense, especially in the light of the association of Tyre and Sidon as sister cities, and as obvious centers of Athirat worship.

14 Gibson, *Canaanite Myths*, p. 91.

15 Gibson, *Canaanite Myths*, p. 91, notes that this is similar to a Sumerian story in which the boy Lugalzaggisi is suckled by the goddess Ninhursag. Perlman, pp. 69-70, comments on the presence of both Athirat and Anat in this text. She says, "It is somewhat unusual to find Athirat and Anat paired, though they appear as wet-nurses of the gods also in UT 52:25, 59, 61 . . . The two goddesses have definite life-giving, or better yet, life sustaining attributes . . . It might be noted though, that while Athirat is the mother of the gods, Anat, outside these texts, has little that we can identify as 'motherly' attributes. We cannot *ipso facto* call these goddesses fertility goddesses. They are life sus-

tainers, those who bless with immortality or advantage, but not really life creators. It is in fact El who, as Keret's personal patron in this text, blesses him and promises him numerous offspring."

16 G. W. Ahlström, *Aspects of Syncretism in Israelite Religion* (Lund: C. W. K. Gleerup, 1963), p. 69.

17 Krt A 145-146. See Chapter 2 for the text.

18 Perlman, *Asherah and Astarte*, pp. 81-83, 86.

19 Gibson, *Canaanite Myths*, pp. 123-24.

Chapter 2

Other Similar Deities

There are several goddesses of the ancient near east that are similar to Asherah. This chapter is a brief examination of the characteristics of a select few of them.[1] It begins with a section dealing with goddesses found in the Ugaritic texts, goddesses similar to Asherah. They include Astarte, Anat, Elath, and Qodesh. The argument will be that the first two, Astarte and Anath, are similar enough to Asherah that the ancient writers occasionally confused them with each other. Elath and Qodesh can be identified as Asherah herself.

The second section of this chapter deals with goddesses found in cultures other than Ugarit, including Ishtar, Ashratu/Ashertu, Atargatis, Tannit, and Isis. Because of their cultural distance from Ugarit, these goddesses will be treated more briefly. It should be noted, however, that they are similar enough to Asherah to catch one's attention and suggest that the mother-goddess is typical of the ancient near east. Asherah can in some ways be identified with the goddesses of these other cultures.

1. Goddesses Found in the Ugaritic Texts

A. Astarte

Astarte is important to this study because she was a mother-goddess and a fertility figure who was similar to Asherah. They were occasionally confused with each other.

There is a large and important study of Astarte (*ʿṯtrt*) in Ugaritic literature by Alice L. Perlman.[2] Much of what follows derives from her study.

Astarte appears infrequently in the Ugaritic texts, much less often than Asherah. Examples follow.

III AB B 40-41[3]

[ymnh.ʿn]t.tủḫd.	Anat took his right hand
šmảlh.tủḫd.ʿṯtrt.	Athtart took his left hand, saying:
ỉk[.]m[ḫṣt.ml][ảk.ym]	How is it that you smite the messengers of Yam?

Baal was defending Yam, the sea god. Anat, Baal's sister, and Athtart (*ʿṯtrt*), were supporting Baal. Athtart's mention here was one of her rare appearances in the Ugaritic texts. Astarte and Anat appear in these verses in parallel form. For the reasons stated in Chapter 1, Section 3, there is little reason to suspect that they are one and the same goddess.

In the next text, Athtart is encouraging Baal to slay Yam and to thereby become king, which he later did.

III AB A 28[4]

bšm.tgʿrm.ʿṯtrt.	Athtart rebuked the Name, saying:
bṯ lảlỉyn.[bʿl]	"Scatter him, O mightiest Baal!"

In the undatable epic of King Keret, Keret was being told in a dream of the beauty of the maiden, Huray, whom he would seek in marriage. This text was quoted and annotated above in Chapter 1, Section 3. Similar to III AB B 40-41 above, the parallel does not necessarily indicate identity.

KRT A 145-146[5]

dk.n m.ʿnt.nʿmh	whose grace is the grace of Anat,
km.tsm.ʿṯtrt.ts[mh]	And her fairness as the fairness of Athtart.

In offering texts[6] Astarte appears with other Ugaritic deities as the recipient of animal offerings. The rituals are not mentioned, only the fact that there were the offerings.[7]

In ritual texts[8] there are announcements of the arrival of Astarte at the palace. In 2004.10 she is called *ʿṯtrt.šd*, Athtart of the field. Perlman[9] argued that this is a fertility/field designation, not a war/field designation, since *šd* in Ugaritic often means cultivated land. In 5:1 she is called *ʿṯtrt.hr*, Hurrian Athtart. Perlman[10] pointed out that this is Hurrian Ishtar, Ishtar of Nineveh, who was later adopted by the Hittites, as argued by de Moor.[11] Perlman suggested that these texts were part of a kingship renewal ceremony since Ishtar was the Mesopotamian deity who bestowed kingship.[12]

Concerning the cult of Athtart and the relationship of Athtart to Ishtar, Perlman summarized her position as follows:

> Clearly there was an organized cult centered about one or several Astartes . . .[and] the spelling of the goddess' name in syllabic cuneiform demonstrated no clear distinction between Ishtar and Astarte. . .[and] I assume Ishtar and Astarte were considered distinct deities but in the Ugaritic texts delineation is not always clear.[13]

Perlman[14] also observed that Astarte and Anat appeared together commonly in the Ugaritic texts. They appear to be clearly differentiated and neither superior in rank to the other. Both are called huntresses.[15] Astarte especially provides food for the gods, but is probably not the same as the Artemis figure who protects hunters.[16]

In a pantheon list[17] Astarte is presented at the end of the list of the important goddesses, preceded by Asherah and Anat, and ahead of the lesser goddesses. She is not in the list of foreign goddesses in spite of her apparent relationship with Ishtar.

Astarte was not the consort of any male deity in the Ugaritic literature. Perlman[18] showed that Astarte in Ugarit was never paired with a male deity, as were Anat (with Baal) and Asherah (with El). But this may be a local phenomenon in which Anat and Asherah took precedence over Astarte. She is a shadowy figure in the mythic literature. Her inclusion in ritual lists and the cult of Astarte in Ugarit were probably late developments enacted under foreign influence.

There was an Astarte cult in Egypt. Perlman[19] noted that there she was depicted as riding a horse, possessing war-like attributes. She was also a sea goddess. This was during the 19th and 20th dynasties, c1300-1100. Perlman noted that there are some similarities between Egyptian Astarte and Semitic Astarte, but not a complete identity.

Astarte was worshiped in Sidon and Philistia. Kapelrud[20] pointed out that this is evident in I Kg 11:5, 33; II Kg 23:13 and in I Sm 31:10; however, he also noted that in these instances it appears that the biblical witness considers Asherah and Astarte as interchangeable names. Agreeing with this is Albright,[21] who said that while the deities are distinct in Ras Shamra texts, they are fused or at least confused with each other in the Hebrew Bible. Gray also agreed that there is this confusion in the Hebrew Bible. As an example of such an interchangeable identity, he points to an Egyptian sculpture of Astarte which bears the name Anat.[22] Furthermore, there is evidence that in Egypt there was an Astarte cult, complete with priests and prophets.[23]

Athirat can be identified with Astarte of Phoenicia. Gray noted, "*ʿttrt* is, of course, Phoenician Astarte, misvocalized by the Massoretes as Ashtoreth."[24] He said that their worship of Astarte was probably stronger in the first millennium than in the second. He argued this particularly because of her weaker role in the Ras Shamra texts. He associated her with fertility and life, though like her Assyrian counterpart, Ishtar, she also had power over death.

Ringgren[25] has identified a Jeremian figure as Astarte. He said that the Queen of Heaven mentioned in Jeremiah 7:18, 44:17ff is Astarte. He also noted that the Athtar [sic] of the Baal cycle, the deity who succeeded Baal after Baal's death, is identical to Athtart except for the feminine ending -t in Athtart. He suggested that these two are related and that they referred originally to a bisexual or at least sexually indeterminate deity.

Yamashita[26] noted that Ashtoreth (Astarte) occurs 9 times in the Hebrew Bible (Jg 2:13, 10:6; I Sam 7:3-4, 12:10, 31:10; I Kg 11:5, 11:33; II Kg 23:13). All of these occurrences are deuteronomistic passages. She is paired with Baal in five of these (Jg 2:13, 10:6; I Sam 7:3-4, 12:10). Considering that Asherah and Baal were also paired in the Hebrew Bible, as will be clearly identified below in Part II of this study, the conclusion can only be that this is further evidence for a growing confusion between the identities of Asherah and Astarte in the Hebrew Bible.

Thus Astarte appears in the Ugaritic texts as a beautiful maiden. Perlman argued acceptably that she fulfilled a fertility role in the Ugaritic cult and was the recipient of animal offerings. Astarte was a lesser goddess, was never paired with any particular male deity, and was rarely mentioned in the texts.

While Astarte and Asherah were quite distinct in the Ugaritic texts, the various scholars cited above, including Gray, Albright, Kapelrud, and Yamashita, gave evidence or concluded that these two goddesses were not as distinct in the Hebrew Bible as they are in the Ugaritic texts. The reason for this is their overlapping characteristics, that Asherah and Astarte were similar as mother-goddess and fertility-goddess figures.

B. Anat

In contrast to Astarte, Anat (*ʿnt*) appears very frequently in the Ugaritic texts. She is a main character in the Baal Cycle myths. She is a powerful deity, the sister and wife of Baal. As a consort-goddess there was the possibility that she might occasionally be confused with Asherah. This discussion is devoted to revealing her identity in the Ugaritic myths. Here are three examples of the occurrence of her name. In the first it is clear that Anat supervised the household duties of the palace of Baal.

V B 3b-5a[27]

kla̓t.ŧg̔rt bht.ʿnt.	Anat did close the gates of mansion,
wtqry.g̔lmm bšt.g̔r	and she met the pages at the foot of the rock.

She was also, like Baal, a war-like deity:

V B 27b-29[28]

kbrkm.tg̔ll bdm žmr.	as she plunged (her) knees in the blood of the guards,
ḥlqm.bmmʿ.mhrm	(her) skirt in the gore of the warriors,
ʿd.tšbʿ.tmtḫs.bbt	until she was sated with fighting in the house.

Anat was found begging Asherah to intercede before El for permission to construct a palace for Baal:

II AB iii 32b-35[29]

wtʿn btlt.ʿnt	And the virgin Anat answered:
nmgn [u̓]m.rbt.a̓ŧrt.ym	"We will importune (our) mother, dame Athirat of the sea,
[ng̔]ẓ.qnyt.i̓lm	[we] will entreat the creatress of the gods.

Anat served as wife of Baal as well as sister.

There is evidence of a cult of Anat. Gray[30] noted that Anat is represented on a 12th century Bethshan stele. The Egyptian hieroglyphic inscription names her as "Antit queen of Heaven and Mistress of the gods." Ringgren[31] also noted this stele and gave it the same translation.

De Moor stated strongly that

> in Canaan, Asherah was completely absorbed by the figure of the consort of Baal, which must have been better known in this area by the name Anat, Astarte, or possibly also *ba alah*, "mistress," and *malkath hashshamayim*, "queen of the heavens." Thus, it may also be assumed that the worship of Anạt in connection with that of Yahweh in the Jewish colony of Elephantine was, in reality, hardly different from the service of Asherah described here.[32]

Hence the biblical references to the queen of heaven who was worshiped in Egypt (e.g., Jr 44:17-19) are probably indirect references to Anat. Biale[33] agreed with this opinion, although he allowed the possibility that the Jeremiah text might also refer to Astarte.

There are several indirect references to Anat in the Hebrew Bible, not mentioning the deity herself, but including her name in other personal names. Ringgren[34] noted that in Jg 5:6 there is a person named "Shamgar son of Anat." In Josh 19:38 and Jg 1:33 there is a place called Beth-Anat, and then there is the familiar home of the prophet Jeremiah, Anathoth (Jr 1:1).

Ps 45 is an Israelite adaptation of the Canaanite myths about Anat. Goulder [35] saw—and his observation has merit—an association between this nuptial song and the wedding of Baal and Anat (IV AB).

In the 12th century Ramses II himself referred to both Anat and Astarte as his shield, taking advantage of their war-like character.[36]

Patai[37] dated Jeremiah's reference to the queen of heaven 626-621, affirming that it refers to Anat. He also gave evidence that Anat was worshiped in Egypt in the 5th century in the Jewish military community, as well as in the 4th and 3rd centuries in the Jewish exilic communities.

Thus Anat is portrayed in the Ugaritic texts as a main character, in contrast to Astarte who was a minor character. Anat was the sister and wife of Baal. She was a powerful and war-like deity, but was not above begging Athirat for a favor for her beloved Baal.

She was in charge of Baal's household. Gray, Ringgren, de Moor, and others have given evidence that there was a cult of Anat, but its specific nature has not been identified.

C. Elath

Elath, as was observed in the previous chapter, was an appellative which referred to the goddess Asherah in the literature of Ugarit. The word is simply the feminine form of "El," meaning "goddess" in a generic sense, and applied to the one who was "the" goddess, Asherah, who was the consort of "the" god, El. Frank Moore Cross[38] observed that the use of this term to describe Asherah is quite well documented in the south part of Palestine. H. Hamberger[39] has found a coin of Tyre ($_c$240 AD) which depicts the goddess of Tyre and bears the inscription "Elath." Although the date is late, this does suggest at least a memory of the ancient goddess of Tyre, well attested in the parallel clauses of the Ras Shamra texts as Asherah.

D. Qodesh

The name of Qodesh appears in the Ras Shamra texts only a few times. An example is in the following:

II AB ii 31-33[40]

dgy.rbt.ảŧr[t.ym]	[O] fisherman of dame Athirat [of the sea]
qḥ.rŧt.bdk.q[dš]	Take a net in your hand, [Qodesh],
rbt.ʿl.ydm[.ảmrr]	a large one on (your) two hands, [Amrur];

Perlman[41] noted that this name has been translated variously, including: the holy God Amurru of the Amorites, the holy one, the holy one passing, and an appellative to indicate Athirat herself. Scholarly opinion has not yet focused on any one of these as the best rendition of the slightly corrupt texts.

Among those who favor Qodesh (or Qudshu) as another name for Asherah is Cross.[42] He pointed to various Ugaritic texts and an interesting Egyptian relief to make his case. An example:

III AB C 19b-20[43]

ảnk.ỉn bt[.l]y[.km.]ỉlm[.]	I myself have not a house like the gods
[w]ḥẓr[.kbn qd]š	[nor] a court [like the sons of the Holy] one.

Baal was complaining to Asherah that he had no palace. The reference to *qdš*, says Cross, is Asherah. This seems sensible, considering the regular references to the sons of Asherah which appear in the Ugaritic texts, meaning all the gods, as for example in II AB 7.

Thus Qodesh can be identified with Athirat, especially considering Cross' rather convincing argument. The discussion concludes with Edwards and Cross who have both addressed the problem of the confusion of Asherah, Astarte, and Anat with each other.

The 13th century Egyptian relief was explained by I. E. S. Edwards.[44] He described it as a nude goddess standing on a lion, holding one or more serpents, wearing the wig of Hathor. He noted that the inscription contained the names of the three Canaanite goddesses Qudshu, Astarte, and Anat, with Qudshu being the equivalent of Asherah in this triad. He noted also that this three-person inscription below a one-figure relief reveals the confusion among the three. Albright[45] agreed with this interpretation of Qudshu, and said further that he is certain of the identification of this name with Asherah.

Cross[46] was conscious of the confusion among the three principle goddesses of Canaan. In explaining this phenomenon he observed what he referred to as the "double movement" of the cosmic Canaanite deities. As local manifestations of the deity were increasingly differentiated one from another, their identities began

Canaanite deities. As local manifestations of the deity were increasingly differentiated one from another, their identities began to separate and new deities emerged to take their places in the pantheon. For example, Asherah was goddess of Tyre and goddess of Sidon, etc. At the same time there were deities with similar traits and functions, e.g., Asherah, Astarte, and Anat. Such similar deities, even if they were not from the same pantheon, tended to merge with each other and become deities of their own. These two movements, the differentiation of deities from one another and the merging of deities into one another, account for the continuous confusion of deities and the fluidity of their identification in the ancient near east.

Thus the goddesses Astarte and Anat are identified in the literature of Ugarit. They have roles distinct from each other, but are similar in such a way that they could possibly be confused with Asherah by the less discerning worshiper or the unknowledgeable. Furthermore, Qodesh and Elath were found to be representations of Asherah, or simple appellations of the same goddess.

2. Goddesses Not Found in the Ugaritic Texts

Besides the deities in the Ugaritic texts, Asherah shares traits, functions, and in some cases phonetic similarities with goddesses of other pantheons. Since there is speculation that Asherah is a relatively late arrival into the Ugaritic pantheon, it is possible that her background extends to the deities of other peoples. Any direct and complete identification of these deities with Asherah is, of course, impossible. Nevertheless, various scholars suggest that the similarities point to at least a partial identification.

A. Ishtar

Ishtar was a major Akkadian goddess of war and fertility. A depiction of her was found along with other deities on a 3rd millennium Akkadian seal. Describing the seal, Butterworth[47] identified the winged goddess as Ishtar, whose ancestor was probably the Sumerian Queen of Heaven, Ninanna/Innini. He said that Ishtar was distinct from all the other Akkadian goddesses because of her wings, which give her a celestial designation. She is carrying a bunch of dates which were sacred to her consort, Anu, the chief God of their pantheon.

Ishtar was a goddess of both war and fertility. Ringgren[48] noted that as a war-goddess she was favored in Assyria. As a fertility/love-goddess she was favored in the Sumerian culture. She is mentioned in the code of Hammurabi and the *Epic of Gilgamesh* and other Akkadian documents.[49] She was, therefore, versatile, and her popularity is demonstrated by numerous temples erected in her honor.

Ishtar legitimated the Akkadian throne. Ringgren[50] also observed that Ishtar was addressed by Akkadian aspirants to the throne, asking her favor and the bestowal of the kingdom's crown. Ishtar's role as legitimator of the crown was a role played by Asherah in Ugarit, as found in the legend of King Keret.

There is reason to associate Ishtar with Asherah. Yamashita[51] expressed certainty regarding the similarity of Ishtar of Babylon and Asherah, and added that there may even have been some confusion between them in Palestine. He cited the Amarna Tablets,[52] letters 60 - 65, as containing variations of the personal name of an important chieftan, *Abdi-Aširti*, which shows confusion between Ishtar, Asherah, and even Astarte. Patai[53] identified Ishtar directly with Asherah, claiming that they are one and the same.

The recently discovered archives of Ebla[54] show that $_c$2500 the goddess Ishtar was familiar to the Eblaite community. The eleventh month of their calendar was dedicated to her and her feast. Ebla, as is now known, had a major trade link with Ugarit. It is likely that knowledge of Ishtar passed from the Sumero-Akkadian territories through Ebla to Ugarit.

Thus, it can be seen that the Akkadian goddess, Ishtar, bears traits similar to Asherah. She was also a fertility/love goddess and the legitimator of the crown. It is possible that the Canaanite knowledge of Asherah was somehow carried to Ugarit from the Akkadians, who knew her as Ishtar.

B. Ashratu/Ashertu

The chief god of the Amorites was Amurru, whose consort was Ashratu, whom Cross[55] identified without hesitation as the counterpart of Canaanite Asherah, just as Amurru is the counterpart of Canaanite El. Yamashita[56] agreed with the identification of Asherah and Amorite Ashratu. He also noted that there was a Hittite goddess with a name similar to Ashratu. Her name was Ashertu and she, like Asherah, was the consort of the Hittite chief god, Elkunirsha. Yamashita identified Ashertu as a close counterpart of Asherah and suggested further that she was Asherah, though with a name whose vocalization is slightly modified.

C. Atargatis

Atargatis was a goddess known from the 4th to 1st century in Syria. Yamashita[57] cited Albright[58] and noted that it is commonly accepted that her name is a combination of the two names Ashtart and Ate (Anat). This notion is confirmed by Miller[59] and by Oden,[60] who added Asherah's name to the list of the deities combined to become Atargatis. He said that Atargatis shared the character and traits of all three deities. As such she was likened to the Greek Hera. She is often depicted riding or standing on lions.[61]

D. Tannit

Tannit was a goddess at Carthage. Cross[62] noted that in recent discussion she has been identified with all three Canaanite deities: Asherah, Astarte, and Anat. However because of her maritime connections and her role as consort of Carthage's god El, he is certain that Asherah is the only appropriate counterpart of Tannit. Tannit is identified with serpents and is often pictured standing on a lion's back.[63] Oden[64] agreed with the identification of Asherah and Tannit, and added that her role as a mother further supports Tannit's close association with the goddess, Asherah. Stager suggested that Tannit and Ashtart were treated as a hypostasis, considering the representations on a seventh century Phoenecian plaque.[65] Olyan, however, seems sure that it is Asherah, not Ashtart.[66]

E. Isis

Isis was the great mother-goddess of Egypt, the goddess of the Nile. She suckled and reared the great Horus, who was her son. Since every Pharaoh of Egypt was seen as the incarnation of Horus, therefore every Pharaoh was a son of Isis. In this role she bore some similarity to Asherah, the goddess who guaranteed the crown of Ugarit and suckled its wearers. Her marine association with the Nile and her nature as a mother-goddess also make her similar to Asherah.

The first group considered was Anat, Astarte, Elath, and Qodesh, all from the Ugaritic texts. While Astarte and Anat were found to be distinctive in the Ugaritic literature, they are nonetheless similar enough to each other to justify the confusion which existed between them and Asherah a few centuries later in the Hebrew Bible. Elath and Qodesh were found not to be individual deities, but rather other names for Asherah herself.

The second group included non-Ugaritic goddesses of the ancient near east who bear similarities to Asherah. Akkadian Ishtar is similar to Asherah in that she was a fertility goddess and a legitimator of the throne. Oden showed that Syrian Atargatis can be partly identified with Asherah. Carthaginian Tannit is an especially good candidate for identification with Asherah because of her role as a maritime protectress, her role as consort of Carthage's chief god, El, and her role as a mother-goddess. She, too, stood on a lion's back. As mother-goddess, the one who suckled kings, and a marine goddess, Isis of Egypt is another deity rather easily compared to Asherah. The similarity of these goddesses to Asherah leads one to conclude that either Asherah was in some way derived from them, or that the character of this deity was so typical and universal in the ancient near east that her appearance in Ugarit, and later among the Israelites, was inevitable.

Notes

1 The more one researches, the longer grows the list of goddesses in the Ancient Near East who were similar in character to Asherah, or whose names were cognates of Asherah. Because of its breadth and depth, the subject matter of this chapter would be the proper object of a major study of its own. The limitations of the present study permit no more than a summary and partial treatment of only a select few of the deities similar to Asherah.

2 Alice Lenore Perlman, *Asherah and Astarte in the Old Testament and Ugaritic Literatures*, a dissertation for the Graduate Theological Union, Berkeley, California (Ann Arbor: University Microfilms International, 1979), pp. 129-182.

3 J. C. L. Gibson, *Canaanite Myths and Legends*, 2nd ed. (Edinburgh: T. & T. Clark, 1978), p. 42.

4 Gibson, *Canaanite Myths*, p. 44.

5 Gibson, *Canaanite Myths*, p. 86.

6 Cyrus H. Gordon, *Ugaritic Textbook*, Analecta Orientalia, no. 38 (Rome: Pontifical Biblical Institute, 1965), no. 19, 22, 23, 1004, 1088, 1091, 2158.

7 Perlman, *Asherah and Astarte*, pp. 130-133.

8 Gordon, *Ugaritic Textbook*, no. 5, 2004.

9 Perlman, *Asherah and Astarte*, pp. 134-135.

10 Perlman, *Asherah and Astarte*, p. 134.

11 J. C. de Moor, "Studies in the New Alphabetic Texts from Ras Shamra II," *Ugarit-Forschungen* 2 (1970): 310.

12 Perlman, *Asherah and Astarte*, p.139.

13 Perlman, *Asherah and Astarte*, p. 140.

14 Perlman, *Asherah and Astarte*, p. 153.

15 Gordon, *Ugaritic Textbook*, no. 2001:2, 124:10.

16 Perlman, *Asherah and Astarte*, p. 156.

17 Gordon, *Ugaritic Textbook*, no. 17; and Perlman, *Asherah and Astarte*, pp. 162-7.

18 Perlman, *Asherah and Astarte*, p. 170.

19 Perlman, *Asherah and Astarte*, pp. 191-202.

20 Arvid S. Kapelrud, *The Ras Shamra Discoveries and the Old Testament*, trans. G. W. Anderson (Tulsa, Oklahoma: University of Oklahoma Press, 1963), p. 64.

21 William Foxwell Albright, *Archaeology and the Religion of Israel* (Baltimore: Johns Hopkins Press, 1942), p. 71.

22 John Gray, *Near Eastern Mythology* (New York: Hamlyn Publishing Group, 1969), p. 74.

23 James B. Pritchard, ed., *Ancient Near Eastern Texts Relating to the Old Testament*, 3rd ed. with supp. (New Jersey: Princeton University Press, 1969), p. 250.

24 John Gray, *The KRT Text in the Literature of Ras Shamra*, 2nd ed. (Leiden: E. J. Brill, 1964), pp. 78-9.

25 Helmer Ringgren, *Religions of the Ancient Near East*, trans. John Sturdy (Philadelphia: Westminster Press, 1973), pp. 141-2.

26 Tadanori Yamashita, *The Goddess Asherah*, a dissertation for Yale University (Ann Arbor: University Microfilms International, 1964), pp. 129-30.

27 Gibson, *Canaanite Myths*, p. 47. For a fuller treatment of Anat, see U. Cassuto, *The Goddess Anath*, trans. Israel Abrahams (Jerusalem: Magnes Press, Hebrew University, 1971).

28 Gibson, *Canaanite Myths*, p. 48.

29 Gibson, *Canaanite Myths*, p. 58.

30 John Gray, *The Canaanites*, in "Ancient Peoples and Places," no. 38 (London: Thames and Hudson, 1964), p. 124.

31 Ringgren, *Religions of the ANE*, p. 142.

32 J. C. de Moor, "Asherah," in *Theological Dictionary of the Old Testament*, vol. 1, eds. G. Johannes Botterweck and Helmer Ringgren (Grand Rapids: William B. Eerdmans, 1979), p. 444.

33 David Biale, "The God with Breasts: El Shaddai in the Bible," *History of Religions* 20 (1982): 255.

34 Ringgren, *Religions of the ANE*, p. 142.

35 Michael D. Goulder, *The Psalms of the Sons of Korah*, Journal for the Study of the Old Testament Supplement Series, no. 20 (Sheffield, England: JSOT Press, 1982), pp. 251-252.

36 Pritchard, *ANE Texts*, p.250.

37 Raphael Patai, *The Hebrew Goddess* (New York: Avon, Discus Book, 1978), pp. 57-8.

38 In Lachish: Frank Moore Cross, "The Evolution of the Proto-Canaanite Alphabet," *Bulletin of the American School of Oriental Research* 134 (1954): 20; "The Origin and Early Evolution of the Alphabet," *Eretz Israel* 8 (1967): p. 16. He also noted that her name appears on later coins of Ascalon, but does not document these.

39 H. Hamberger, "A Hoard of Syrian Tratacrachms and the Tyrian Bronze Coins from Gush Halav," *Israel Exploration Journal* 4 (1954): 208, 224 (no. 138), and pl. 21.

40 Gibson, *Canaanite Myths*, p. 57.

41 Perlman, *Asherah and Astarte*, pp. 80-81.

42 Frank Moore Cross, *Canaanite Myth and Hebrew Epic* (Cambridge: Harvard University Press, 1973), pp. 20, 33-4.

43 Gibson, *Canaanite Myths*, p. 38.

44 I. E. S. Edwards, "A Relief of Qudshu-Astarte-Anath in the Winchester College Collection," *Journal of Near Eastern Studies* 14 (1955): 49-51. It is also pictured in James B. Pritchard, *The Ancient Near East in Pictures Relating to the Old Testament*, 2nd ed. with supp. (New Jersey: Princeton University Press, 1969), p. 473 along with three others which are quite similar, plates 471-472, and 474.

45 William Foxwell Albright, *Yahweh and the Gods of Canaan: A Historical Analysis of Two Contrasting Faiths* (London: Athlone Press, 1968), pp. 121, 146.

46 Cross, *Canaanite Myth*, p. 49.

47 E. A. S. Butterworth, *The Tree at the Navel of the Earth* (Berlin: Walter de Gruyter, 1970), pp. 68-9.

48 Ringgren, *Religions of the ANE*, pp. 60-1.

49 Pritchard, *ANE Texts*, pp. 604-7.

50 Ringgren, *Religions of the ANE*, pp. 100-1.

51 Yamashita, *The Goddess*, pp. 16-22.

52 J. A. Knudtzon, *Die El-Amarna Tafeln*, 2 vols. (Leipzig: J. C. Hinrichs'sche Buchhandlung, 1908-1915).

53 Patai, *Hebrew Goddess*, p. 20.

54 Giovanni Pettinato, *The Archives of Ebla: An Empire Inscribed in Clay* (New York: Doubleday, 1981), pp. 150, 257.

55 Cross, *Canaanite Myth*, p. 57.

56 Yamashita, *The Goddess*, pp, 3-7, 31-44. There is evidence of an Ashratum in Babylon, but William L. Reed, *The Asherah in the Old Testament* (Fort Worth: Texas Christian University, 1949), pp. 72-3 is clear that she migrated to Babylon from the Amorites and did not take the place of Ishtar.

57 Yamashita, *The Goddess*, pp. 97-99.

58 William Foxwell Albright, "The Evolution of the West-Semitic Divinity ʻAN-ʻANAT-ʻATTA," *American Journal of Semitic Languages and Literatures* 41 (1925): 88.

59 Patrick D. Miller, Jr., "Ugarit and the History of Religions," *Journal of Northwest Semitic Languages* 9 (1981): 124.

60 R. A. Oden, Jr., *Studies in Lucian's "De Syria Dea"*, Harvard Semitic Museum, no. 15 (Missoula Montana: Scholars Press, 1977), pp. 47-105.

61 Oden, *Studies in Lucian*, pp. 52-3. See Chapter 9 for references associating Asherah and lions.

62 Cross, *Canaanite Myth*, pp. 28-33.

63 Cross, "Origin," p. 13.

64 Oden, *Studies in Lucian*, pp. 92-3.

65 L. Stager and S. Wolff. "Child Sacrifice at Carthage, Religious Rite or Population Control?" *Biblical Archaeology Review* 10 (1984):31-51.

66 Saul M. Olyan. *Asherah and the Cult of Yahweh in Israel*, SBL Monograph Series, No. 34, (Atlanta, Georgia: Scholars Press, 1988), p. 60.

PART II

ASHERAH IN THE HEBREW BIBLE

Who was Asherah to the ancient Hebrews? The primary evidence lies in the 40 texts of the Hebrew Bible which mention Asherah. She was, despite the biblical prohibitions, a deity adopted from the Canaanites and worshiped along with Yahweh, even as the consort of Yahweh. There was a major cult of Asherah worship among the Israelites. Her cult symbol, the post, was placed near the altar in the Temple. Under her auspices, there was a group of male prostitutes which operated in the Temple precincts. While Asherah worship was widespread and at times officially endorsed, it was also hated by the deuteronomistic theologian.

Chapter 3

Overview of the Texts

Chapter 3 is a broad overview of the texts, attempting to show the general picture of Asherah as found in the Hebrew Bible. The discussion includes the major contributions to Asherah studies from the last few decades, which is dominated by three persons, William L. Reed, Tadanori Yamashita, and Alice L. Perlman.

Following this review is a tabular analysis of the Asherah texts, showing the results of comparing the use of Asherah with four other terms found in the Asherah texts. These terms are divided into nine usage groups, called formulas. After this categorization, these usage groups are considered as a whole, from which emerges a "meta-formula," a term which will be explained below. This meta-formula has special significance for the use of the term Asherah.

1. The Texts

Asherah appears in the Hebrew Bible in 40 verses: Ex 34:13; Dt 7:5, 12:3, 16:21; Jg 3:7, 6:25, 6:26, 6:28, 6:30; I Kg 14:15, 14:23, 15:13, 16:33, 18:19; II Kg 13:6, 17:10, 17:16, 18:4, 21:3, 21:7, 23:4, 23:6, 23:7, 23:14, 23:15; II Ch 14:2, 15:16, 17:6, 19:3, 24:18, 31:1, 33:3, 33:19, 34:3, 34:4, 34:7; Is 17:8, 27:9; Jr 17:2, and Mi 5:13.[1] It occurs 18 times in the singular, of these 6 without the definite article and 12 with the definite article. It occurs in the plural form 'asheroth' 3 times, of these 1 without the definite article and 2 with. It occurs in the plural form 'asherim' 19 times, of these 3 without the definite article, 10 with the definite article, and 6 times with suffixes.[2]

2. Review of the Literature

A. Early Attempts

The first extensive modern study of Asherah in the Hebrew Bible was completed as recently as 1949 by William L. Reed.[3] In this study Reed noted that the earlier explanations of Asherah fall into three categories. First, there were those who said that Asherah is either the goddess Ashtaroth (Astarte) or her cult object. Second, there were those who said that the Asherah is a cult object for a deity who is not identified. Third, there were those who interpreted Asherah as a cult object, and a goddess whose name is Asherah, not Astarte or any other.[4]

The spokesman for the first group is Max Ohnefalsch-Richter.[5] His 1893 book considered, in the course of examining Cypriot archaeology, the identity of the Asherah in the Hebrew Bible. Since the Asherah in the Hebrew Bible is frequently represented as a wooden pole, Ohnefalsch-Richter contended that various scenes in Cypriot art depicting trees and wooden poles might also be called Asherahs. Moreover, Ohnefalsch-Richter assumed that Ashtaroth and Asherah were the same deity despite the obvious philological difference in the names. Thus he concluded that the poles of both Cyprus and the Hebrew Bible were representations of Ashtaroth and her cult objects. Judgment against Ohnefalsch-Richter's untenable position should be mitigated by observing that the Ras Shamra texts were not available in 1893, and that the existence of a goddess named Asherah was, in his time, purely conjectural.[6]

Representative of the second group, those who claim that Asherah is a cult object and not a deity, are W. Robertson Smith and Karl Budde.[7] Often cited by these scholars are the texts such as Dt. 16:21, which speaks of the planting of the wooden Asherah beside the altar without any reference to a particular deity, perhaps as a replacement for the live tree under which the most ancient of altars were built, and II Kg 13:6, in which Jehu was cleansing the Samarian sanctuary of all the Tyrian deities, but nevertheless left the Asherah standing, a curious omission, understandable only if it can be assumed that the Asherah was not a deity. Their arguments do not take into sufficient account the passages wherein Asherah seems to be a name, e.g. II Kg 23:4. Dismissing them as late additions, they deny that these texts are relevant.

The third group, those who claim that Asherah is both a cult object and a deity with the same name, is represented in early scholarship by A. Kuenen and G. W. Collins.[8] The defense for this position is based on the biblical evidence. In some passages the Hebrew Bible refers to a wooden object, e.g., Dt 16:21, and in other passages it makes Asherah the name of a deity, e.g. I Kg 15:13. Further evidence comes from passages such as II Kg 21:3, 21:7, and 23:6 wherein the cult object is first called an Asherah and then the image of Asherah, leading one to assume that when an object is an image of a deity which is outside the object itself, then the deity bears the name assigned to the object. This was a bold assumption, much more credible in modern generations after the discovery of the Ras Shamra texts, which for the first time gave the world certainty that there really had been a goddess named Asherah in the Canaanite pantheon.[9] The position of this third group has become the only position pursued by serious scholarship today.

B. Reed

Reed's study was the first major study about Asherah after the discovery of the Ras Shamra texts. He has laid the foundations for all further Asherah research. A significant part of his study is an observation of the verbs used in connection with Asherah.[10] Reed maintained that these verbs give clues to the meaning of Asherah in the Hebrew Bible.

First citing five verbs, Reed suggested that Asherah was an object constructed by humans: *ʿsh* (to make or fashion) in I Kg 14:15, 15:13, 16:33; II Kg 17:16, 21:3, 21:7; II Ch 15:16, 33:3; Is 17:8; *bnh* (to build or construct) in I Kg 14:23; *ʿmd* (to stand erect) in II Kg 13:6, II Ch 33:19; *nṣb* (to set up or erect) in II Kg 17:10; and *ntʿ* (to plant or fix in place) in Dt 16:21. From the Hebrew Bible's use of these verbs, Reed reached three conclusions. First, the Asherah was not an object that occurred naturally like a tree or a grove of trees. Second, the Asherah was constructed by humans and used in cultic worship which was represented as reprehensible to the Lord. Third, this object stood erect as opposed to lying down.

Reed next cited ten verbs used with Asherah in the Hebrew Bible when the intent of the story is to tell of the destruction of the Asherahs: *krt* (to cut off or cut down) in Ex 34:13; Jg 6:25, 6:26, 6:30; II Kg 18:4, 23:14; *gdʿ* (to cut off or destroy) in Dt. 7:5; II Ch 14:2, 31:1; *srp* (to burn or burn down) in Dt 12:13; II Kg 23:6, 23:15; *bʿr* in the Piel (to consume or burn or remove) in II Ch 19:3; *sbr* (to break to pieces) in II Ch 34:7; *ntṣ* (to overturn) in II Ch 34:3; *dqq* (to pulverize) in II Ch 34:4; II Kg 23:6; *ntš* (to pluck up) in Mi 5:14; *yṣʾ* (to remove) in II Kg 23:6; and *hsr* (to remove or take away) in II Ch 17:6.

Noting that in II Kg 23:4 the dissolution of Asherah worship included the vessels used in the service of Asherah, Reed suggested that there were cultic rituals observed in the service of Asherah. The identity of this Asherah is suggested in this same verse when the name Asherah is placed in parallel with the name Baal. Baal is a god; Asherah is, therefore, a goddess.

Reed concluded his verb study convinced that he had shown Asherah as both a cult object and a deity. He observed that all the verbs used with Asherah would apply if the cult object was thought of as an image. This leaves open the possibility that worship of the Asherah could have referred to worship of the goddess who bore that name.

The next task was a noun study.[11] The objects most frequently associated with Asherah are: *mizbēah* (altar) in Ex 34:13; Dt 7:5[12]; *bāmāh* (high place) in I Kg 14:23; II Kg 17:10; *maṣṣēbāh* (pillar) in Ex 34:13; Dt 7:5; *pesel* (graven image) in Dt 7:5; II Kg 21:7; and *hammānīm* (incense altars) in II Ch 14:4; Is 17:8.

Regarding the altar, Reed noted that the Hebrew Bible, while encouraging the destruction of Canaanite altars and of Asherahs, is attempting to prevent the erection of an Asherah next to the altar of the Lord (Dt 16:21). The implication is that the Asherah was peculiar to the worship of a particular deity, while the altar could be validly used in the worship of various deities, including Yahweh.

It is apparent that the Asherah object was so directly related to the deity herself that its use could not be adapted to Yahwistic service. This same argument applies to the Judges 6 passage about Gideon, who destroyed the Canaanite altar and the Asherah and built a new altar but no Asherah to the Lord. This and several other passages (II Kg 21:3; II Ch 33:3, 34:4) indicates that there is a direct association between the altar of Baal and the Asherah object. This suggests that the devotion was to a divine pair, Baal and his consort Asherah.

Avoiding a large-scale inquiry into the nature of the high places, Reed did observe, though, that in the eleven passages where the Asherah and the high place both occur (all in the books of Kings and Chronicles) the high place is a sanctuary which appears with the Asherah as an accessory of Canaanite worship. The Hebrew Bible disapproves of these both and speaks against their use.

The stone pillar is mentioned eleven times in the same texts with the Asherah. However, in these same texts are included other cult objects. Though their columnar shape is similar to that of the Asherahs, Reed noted that the texts do not allow one to conclude that the function of the pillar is similar to the function of the Asherah. While one might be inclined to suggest that the pillar represents the male deity and the Asherah the female, no such interpretation is justified by the Hebrew Bible.

Since the term 'graven image' is used in conjunction with Asherah in eight texts, one might be tempted to conclude that the Asherah is therefore something other than a carved image of a deity. Reed dismissed this thought by arguing that this wooden Asherah was sufficiently dissimilar in appearance from the other carved images that, even though it would technically fall under the category of carved images, it nevertheless merited a name of its own. They were both, however, types of carved images. Especially in two of these texts (I Kg 15:13, II Kg 21:37) is it obvious that the Asherah is both the name of the deity and the name of the image of the deity, Asherah.

In a brief treatment of incense altars Reed dismissed the four instances when they are mentioned with Asherah, saying that they have no relationship to Asherah. This contention must be re-examined in the light of the archaeological discoveries treated later in the present study.

Giving special attention to the Elijah story of the contest with the prophets of Baal and the prophets of Asherah (I Kg 18), Reed noted first of all that the prophets of Asherah and those of Baal are mentioned in vs 19 of the MT, indicating their presence at the event, yet only the prophets of Baal are later mentioned in vş 22 as having participated in the contest. He suggested an accidental omission from the MT as a solution, based on the evidence in the LXX which has the prophets of Asherah in both verses.[13] From the presence of the four hundred prophets of Asherah, Reed suggested that the cult of Asherah was both highly organized and powerful and that she may have been considered as the consort of Baal. Recalling II Kg 23:4 which mentions the vessels made for her and kept in the temple of Jerusalem, he suspected that worship of Asherah was conducted even there.

There are three texts which Reed mentioned as the three places in the Hebrew Bible were Asherah is in some way associated with Yahweh. He did not consider this association a direct one. He claimed that the politically expedient act would have been to place an Asherah object beside the altar of Yahweh, so that her devotees could worship the deity of their choice at one place. In the light of inscriptions and archaeological evidence which has turned up since Reed's study, this position must be reworked. The evidence is presented in later parts of the present study.

Using the dates of many of the Asherah texts of the Hebrew Bible, Reed developed a chronology of Asherah.[14] Since Asherah was adopted from the Canaanites after the Israelites settled in Canaan, one would not expect to find Asherah in any passages dating from before the settlement. This is indeed the case. The event which recounts Asherah for the first time in Kings is found in I Kg 15:33. It describes the tenth century reign of Asa in Judah.[15] The first mention of Asherah in the northern kingdom is I Kg 16:33 during the reign of Ahab. Asherah continued to be mentioned until the beginning of the sixth century (Is 27:9, 17:8; Jer 17:2; Mi

5:14). These dates, Reed cautioned, are not to be considered the outer parameters of Asherah worship amongst the Israelites. The absence of biblical statements outside of these dates does not force any assumptions about the absence of Asherah worship either before or after its recorded presence in the Hebrew Bible. It is easily possible that Asherah worship was happening both before and after the recorded evidence, before the tenth century and after the sixth. Reed did not state, but it is arguable that these dates are not the outer parameters but the inner parameters of Asherah worship by Israel, the smallest possible time period in which Asherah was worshiped, a period which could well be larger than the period datable by evidence from the Hebrew Bible.

C. Yamashita

Another Asherah study worthy of note is by Tadanori Yamashita.[16] In his section about Asherah in the Hebrew Bible, Yamashita advances beyond the work of Reed and raises fresh questions.[17]

An important observation credited to Yamashita is that all forty occurrences of Asherah in the Hebrew Bible are in deuteronomistic passages and passages directly dependent on deuteronomistic texts. Even Ex 34:13 is now recognized by many scholars as deuteronomistic.[18] This leaves no doubt that the major source of the Hebrew Bible's concern to obliterate Asherah worship comes from the era of Josiah's reform.

Asking whether this Asherah is the same Asherah which appears in the Ugaritic texts, Yamashita concluded that it is not. His reasons were these: 1) El, the deity associated with Asherah in the Ugaritic texts was forgotten in the Hebrew Bible. 2) Rather, Asherah is paired with Baal. This does not occur in the Ugaritic texts. 3) Only three of the forty passages in the Hebrew Bible definitely refer to a deity (Jg 3:7; I Kg 18:17; II Kg 23:4). 4) In other passages it is not Baal but the altar of Baal which is paired with Asherah (Jg 6:25, 6:28, 6:30; II Ch 33:3, 34:4). 5) Even in the texts where Asherah is paired with Yahweh (e.g., II Kg 23:7) one must be careful to note that also associated with Yahweh are the sun, the moon, and the heavenly host, thus diluting the specificity of the association of Asherah and Yahweh. 6) While the Ugaritic texts state that the goddess of Tyre and Sidon is Asherah, the Hebrew Bible says it is Ashtoreth (I Kg 11:5, 11:33; II Kg 23:13). 7) Ashtoreth is used nine times in the Hebrew Bible (Jg 2:13, 10:6; I Sam 7:3, 7:4, 12:10, 31:10; I Kg 11:5, 11:33; II Kg 23:13), each time as the name of a goddess.

Yamashita also concluded that the writers of the Hebrew Bible leaned more toward the 'wooden object' notion of Asherah and used 'Ashtoreth' as the usual name of the deity. What he did not envision in his study is the possibility that Asherah might be paired with Baal precisely because Canaanite El is mostly forgotten by the time of the Josian reform, and that a likely assumption from the Hebrew Bible is that Baal has taken El's place as chief of the Canaanite pantheon. All of this took place at least six centuries after the writing of the Ras Shamra texts and thus would not be reflected in those texts.

Another matter neglected by Yamashita is that there was increasing confusion between Asherah and Ashtaroth (Astarte), such that their roles were fusing with one another and their names were beginning to be used interchangeably. These concerns weaken Yamashita's theory that Asherah of the Hebrew Bible had become merely a cultic wooden object and had lost her distinction as a particular deity. It is possbile to argue using the same texts that Yamashita used, e.g., Jg 2:13, I Kg 11:5, that the Hebrew Bible does not give evidence of a marked distinction between Asherah and Astarte. On the contrary, their occurrence in the deuteronomistic texts, in passages referring to the deity, shows that the names were coming to be used interchangeably for the same goddess, the one associated with Baal.

Of further concern is the fact that the Ashtoreth is not used in association with any cult object, but exclusively as a deity. This does not support, as Yamashita supposed, the conclusion that they are different. The absence of references to cult objects in association with Ashtoreth does not mean that there were none. Furthermore, this absence could be explained simply by noting that the confusion of Ashtoreth with Asherah was a later development, and therefore it would not be surprising if the wooden cult object which originally bore the name of the Asherah, the goddess it represented, would continue to bear the same name, if for no other reason than by force of habit, even though the name of the personal deity became confused.

D. Perlman

There is one other major work which deals with Asherah in the Hebrew Bible, namely, the study by Alice L. Perlman.[19] She began with an informative overview of each of the Hebrew texts, showing the form of each Hebrew occurrence of Asherah. However, she suggested that the word Asherim (*ʿšrym*) is lexically separate from Asherah and therefore distinct from the name of the goddess Asherah. She said that the Asherah (feminine singular) refers to objects made by humans which were established by the apostate kings or to the goddess as in the Ahab-Jezebel texts (e.g. II Kg 17:9ff, 21:3ff; II Ch 37:3), whereas Asherim (masculine plural) appears most frequently in expressions which describe the religious reforms of the Judahite kings, especially referring to the destruction of the objects. Perlman then began an analysis of these expressions, showing how they derive from Pentateuchal law, especially Ex 34:13, Dt 7:5, and Dt 12:3.

These expressions, Perlman stated, appear to be a patterned formula. It is a stable and regular pattern which describes the action taken against the foreign cult objects. While the pattern is stable, its content changes a little from text to text. The changes are due to the use of variable components, supplied mostly from the deuteronomistic lists of cult objects which are condemned by the law, and verbs describing the appropriate actions to be taken against these objects (Dt 7 and 12). Perlman's assumption was that the three Pentateuchal expressions are the original models used as a pattern by the deuteronomistic redactors of the historical books, whenever they needed to express action taken against foreign cult objects. Their known loyalty to the deuteronomic law serves to support such an assumption, as well as the texts themselves, which show great similarity to each other and to the deuteronomic format.

There are three occurrences of the word Asherim in the Pentateuch (Ex 34:13, Dt 7:5, and Dt 12:3). In each case the context describes some command to eliminate the foreign cult objects. Perlman observed that the word Asherah occurs only once in the Pentateuch (Dt 16:21), which is an admonition against erecting an Asherah and other objects which she described as "monuments" to other gods.[20] Her suggestion was, then, that with only a few exceptions, when they are being torn down these cult objects are Asherim, and when they are being set up they are monuments to Asherah. This, if it were demonstrated as true, would show that the two terms are lexically separate and have separate meanings.

Perlman is vulnerable in this matter. The evidence which she offered does not show that Asherim and Asherah are lexically separate. Her attempt to separate the terms, Asherah being a monument to a goddess, and Asherim being simply a cult object not representing a goddess, is difficult to maintain in the light of the following arguments.

1) In the four verses of the Pentateuch which use some form of Asherah, the pertinent nouns used along with Asherah in these verses are altar (*mizbēah*), pillar (*maṣṣēbāh*), and idol (*pesel*). In three of the four verses, all the forms are plural, including Asherim: Ex 34:13 has altars, pillars, and Asherim; Dt 7:5 has altars, pillars, Asherim and idols; Dt 12:3 has altars, pillars, and Asherim. In the other one of the four verses, the forms are singular: Dt 16:21 has pillar, Asherah, and altar. Given these facts, the argument proceeds as follows.

2) Perlman saw in these verses a lexical separation. She did not realize that there is an easier explanation, that is, that all there is here is a simple difference caused by the use of the singular form in one instance and the plural in the others. These are the singular and plural of the same noun.

3) The substitution of this simpler argument for Perlman's more complex argument is defensible if the context of the texts is able to offer an explanation for the use of the singular in one instance and

the plural in others. Such an explanation can be shown. The three instances when the plural is used are texts in which there is admonishment against widespread syncretism. These texts refer in a general way to the many places where these Asherahs and other objects had been illicitly erected and which should, therefore, be torn down by the reformers. Since there were so many of them it was natural to refer to them, the Asherahs included, in the plural forms. The context of Dt 16, however, is different from these other three texts. The point of reference is not the multiplication of foreign cult objects in the territory, but rather the abominable practices in the central site, the temple of Yahweh. One of the primary emphases of the deuteronomic reform was the centralized cult at the Jerusalem temple. Thus the deuteronomistic sources would not be speaking of more than one genuine location for the service of Yahweh. Since there may be only one cult site, then there may be only one altar (singular). While the illicit worship sites may each have had an altar, a pillar, and an Asherah, totalling many of each (plural), the abomination to be avoided at the central cult site would have been only one of each (singular). There is, therefore, no basis in these texts for suggesting different meanings for the singular and plural forms of Asherah. On the contrary, these texts reinforce their similarity by the parallel constructions, and hearken back to Reed's affirmation that the Asherah in the Hebrew Bible is both a cult object and an image of the goddess Asherah. The Asherah and the Asherim are lexically the same.

4) The exceptions to Perlman's supposed pattern of using Asherah to refer only to the monuments to the deity and Asherim to refer to the cult object further dilute her arguments. There are more than the few she claimed. There are eight exceptions, that is, in one out of every five times when Asherah/Asherim is used it does not follow her pattern. Three of the exceptions refer to the Asherim as being constructed, an act which Perlman said is reserved for the goddess word Asherah (I Kg 14:23; II Kg 17:10; II Ch 33:19). The other five exceptions refer to the Asherah being torn down, an act which Perlman reserves for the cult-object word Asherim (II Kg 18:4, 23:6, 23:15; Jg 6:28, 6:30). When one fifth of

the occurrences are at variance from the norm, one should hesitate calling them exceptions. Moreover, the norm itself is called into question. It is difficult to maintain that there is a lexical pattern which distinguishes between the Asherah and the Asherim when in so many instances the texts do not hold true to the pattern.

5) These "exceptions" can be adequately explained by recalling the principle of argument 3 above. The use of Asherah-Asherim in seven of the eight texts comes clear in considering the context. When the text is referring to the multiplicity of cult sites, it does not seem to matter whether the Asherah/Asherim are being erected or destroyed. What matters is simply that there are many of them. In these instances the plural form is used (I Kg 14:23; II Kg 17:10; II Ch 33:19). When the text refers to a single cult site (in these instances either Ophrah or Jerusalem), specifically a Hebrew altar, it again appears that little or no attention is paid to whether the Asherah is being erected or destroyed. In these texts the point of reference is the single cult site. Therefore, the singular form is used (Jg 6:28, 6:30; II Kg 23:6, 23:15). This argument is not jeopardized by the one exception, II Kg 18:4, which uses a singular form of Asherah in the context of the destruction of the many cult sites, including the destruction of their high places and pillars. The singular here (*haʿashērāh*) appears to be a textual variant, corrected and made properly plural in the LXX (*tà ʾálsē*). It is also found in the plural in the Syriac, Sperber's Targum, and the Vulgate.

Thus Perlman's contention that Asherah and Asherim are lexically distinct is untenable. She failed to recognize a simpler explanation for the pattern, the explanation that the use of singular and plural forms is determined by the context, the plural being used when the text refers to the multiple cult sites and the singular being used when the text refers to a single cult site. This is all the more evident when considering the number of exceptions. According to Perlman's pattern, eight significant exceptions emerge. By the pattern suggested in the present study, only one exception is noted, and that exception is not significant.

Another aspect of Perlman's work, however, has proved to be especially valuable. She observed that there is a formulaic pattern which usually surrounds the use of Asherah-related words.[21] She has described this pattern as stable in form but variable in vocabulary. However, since her work is based largely on the invalid assumption that Asherah and Asherim are lexically separate, she has mostly ignored the occurrences of Asherah (singular) in her consideration of the formula. Having given Perlman proper credit for the idea of seeing the use of a formula in the Hebrew Bible, it is now necessary to re-examine the existence of that formula, giving consideration to the use of Asherah in all its forms.

3. Tabular Analysis

The following tables present the information necessary for an analysis of the terms used in formulaic construction with Asherah in the Hebrew Bible. There are 4 terms which occur with noticeable frequency in the Asherah texts: carved image (*pesel*), pillar (*maṣṣēbāh*), high place (*bāmāh*), and altar (*mizbēah*). The tables observe from various dimensions the combinations of these terms and their frequence of occurrence.

A. Simple Data

Table 1 contains the information in its simplest form. It is a list of the passages where the terms Asherah, carved image, pillar, and high place are found in the Hebrew Bible. Since the term altar so permeates the Hebrew Bible, it is not helpful to cite its every occurrence. Therefore, altar is listed only when it is found near one or more of the other four terms. Note well, for future reference, that altar is listed arbitrarily on the tables as "L" so as not to duplicate the "A" which designates Asherah.

It should be noted that all five of the terms listed are found in the Hebrew Bible in various modified forms, i.e., in the plural, with suffixes, with prefixes, etc. To keep the tables as uncluttered as possible, no attempt has been made to indicate these modifications, which are in any case of minimal significance in this analysis. Any modifications worthy of note are mentioned in the final section of this chapter.

The citations are arranged on Table 1 in such a way that one can easily observe the terms which are found in combination in a particular verse or set of verses by reading across the page. For example, the first combination can be found in Exodus 34:13 where Asherah, pillar, and altar are used together. These combinations will be further analyzed in Tables 2, 3, 4, and 5, which are all based on the information contained in Table 1. In several instances the same term is found more than once in a given verse. In such cases the number of times it occurs is placed in parentheses next to the citation. For example, high place occurs twice in I Kg 13:33. It is indicated thus: I Kg 13:33(2x).

Table 1, Simple Data

Table 1 presents the citations of every Hebrew Bible text where Asherah, Carved Image (pesel), Pillar (maṣṣēbāh), High Place (bāmāh), and their Hebrew variants occur, as well as each text where Altar (mizbēaḥ) occurs with any of these terms.

	Asherah	Carved Image (pesel)	Pillar (maṣṣēbah)	High Place (bāmāh)	Altar (mizbēaḥ)
GN			28:18		
			28:22		
			31:13		
			31:45		
			31:51		
			31:52		
			35:14		
			35:20		
EX		20:4			20:24
					20:25
			23:24		
			24:4		
	34:13		34:13		34:13

	Asherah	Carved Image (pesel)	Pillar (maṣṣēbah)	High Place (bāmāh)	Altar (mizbēaḥ)
LV		26:1	26:1		
				26:30	
NM				21:19	
				21:20	
				21:28	
				33:52	
DT		4:16			
		4:23			
		4:25			
		5:8			
	7:5	7:5	7:5		7:5
		7:25			
	12:3	12:3	12:3		12:3
	16:21				16:21
			16:22		
		27:15			
				32:13	
				33:29	
JOS				13:17	
JG	3:7				
		3:19			
		3:26			
					6:24
	6:25				6:25
	6:26				6:26
	6:28				6:28
	6:30				6:30
					6:31
					6:32
		17:3			
		17:4			
		18:14			

	Asherah	Carved Image (pesel)	Pillar (maṣṣēbah)	High Place (bāmāh)	Altar (mizbēaḥ)
JG (con't)		18:17			
		18:18			
		18:20			
		18:30			
		18:31			
I SM				9:12	
				9:13	
				9:14	
				9:19	
				9:25	
				10:5	
				10:13	
II SM				1:19	
				1:25	
			18:18		
				22:34	
I KG				3:2	
				3:3	
				3:4	3:4
				11:7	
				12:31	
				12:32	12:32
				13:32	
				13:33(2x)	
	14:15				
	14:23		14:23	14:23	
	15:13				
				15:14	
					16:32
	16:33				
	18:19				
				22:44	

	Asherah	Carved Image (pesel)	Pillar (maṣṣēbah)	High Place (bāmāh)	Altar (mizbēaḥ)
II KG			3:2		
			10:26		
			10:27		
				12:4	
	13:6				
				14:4	
				15:4	
				15:35	
				16:4	
				17:9	
	17:10		17:10		
				17:11	
	17:16				
				17:29	
				17:32(2x)	
		17:41			
	18:4		18:4	18:4	
				18:22	18:22
	21:3			21:3	21:3
					21:4
					21:5
	21:7	21:7			
	23:4				
				23:5	
	23:6				
	23:7				
				23:8	
				23:9	23:9
					23:12
				23:13	
	23:14		23:14		
	23:15			23:15(2x)	23:15(2x)
					23:16

	Asherah	Carved Image (pesel)	Pillar (maṣṣēbah)	High Place (bāmāh)	Altar (mizbēaḥ)
II KG (con't)					23:17
				23:19	
				23:20	23:20
I CH				16:39	
					16:40
				21:29	21:29
II CH				1:3	
					1:5
					1:6
				1:13	
				11:15	
	14:2		14:2	14:2	14:2
				14:3	
					15:8
	15:16				
				15:17	
	17:6			17:6	
	19:3				
				20:33	
				21:11	
	24:18				
				28:4	
				28:25	
	31:1		31:1	31:1	31:1
				32:12	32:12
	33:3			33:3	33:3
					33:4
					33:5
		33:7			
					33:15
					33:16
				33:17	
	33:19	33:19		33:19	

	Asherah	Carved Image (pesel)	Pillar (maṣṣēbah)	High Place (bāmāh)	Altar (mizbēaḥ)
II CH (con't)		33:22			
	34:3	34:3		34:3	
	34:4	34:4			34:4
					34:5
	34:7	34:7			34:7
PS				18:34	
		78:58		78:58	
		97:7			
IS		10:10			
				14:14	
				15:2	
				16:12	
	17:8				17:8
			19:19		19:19
	27:9				27:9
		30:22			
				36:7	
					36:37
		40:19			
		40:20			
		42:8			
		42:17			
		44:9			
		44:10			
		44:15			
		44:17			
		45:20			
		48:5			
				58:14	
JR				7:31	
		8:19			
		10:14			

	Asherah	Carved Image (pesel)	Pillar (maṣṣēbah)	High Place (bāmāh)	Altar (mizbēaḥ)
JR (con't)					17:1
	17:2				17:2
				17:3	
				19:5	
				26:18	
				32:35	
			43:13		
				48:35	
		50:38			
		51:17			
		51:47			
		51:52			
EZ				6:3	
					6:4
					6:5
				6:6	6:6
				16:16	
				20:29(2x)	
			26:11		
				36:2	
				43:7	
HO			3:4		
			10:1		10:1
			10:2		10:2
					10:5
				10:8	10:8
		11:2			
JB				9:8	
AM				4:13	
				7:9	

	Asherah	Carved Image (pesel)	Pillar (maṣṣēbah)	High Place (bāmāh)	Altar (mizbēaḥ)
MI				1:3	
				1:5	
		1:7			
				3:12	
		5:12	5:12		
	5:13				
NA		1:14			
HB		2:18			
				3:19	

B. All Possible Combinations

The information of Table 1 becomes more useful as it is further described. Table 2 is a list of every possible combination of the five terms. Each combination is annotated with the number of times it can be found in the Hebrew Bible and followed by its exact locations in the Hebrew texts. In the instance that a term appears more than once in a passage, as in the case of Asherah, carved image, and high place in II Ch 33:19, such is noted after the citation.

One can observe immediately that some of the citations include more than one verse. The author considers several verses as single texts if the verses in question are by sense harmonious and not separated from each other either by other ideas or literary interruptions. For example, Dt 16:21 reads "You shall not plant a sacred pole [Asherah] of any kind of wood beside the altar of the Lord, your God, which you will build." Then immediately following it, Dt 16:22 reads "nor shall you erect a sacred pillar, such as the Lord, your God, detests." In vs. 21 the terms Asherah and altar appear, and in vs 22 the term pillar. It is obvious that the verses belong together as a unit. Therefore, this citation will be found listed under the combination of terms "APL."

Table 2, All Possible Combinations

Table 2 presents the combinations of Asherah (A), Carved Image (C), Pillar (P), High Place (H), and Altar (L) as they are found in the Hebrew Bible texts where they are used together. Each is used once per text unless indicated otherwise.

AC (none)

ACP (1)
MI 5:12-13

ACPH (none)

ACPHL (none)

ACPL (2)
DT 7:5
DT 12:3

ACH (1)
II CH 33:19
A C (2x) H

ACHL (3)
II KG 21:3-7
II CH 33:3-7
A C H L(3x)
II CH 34:3-5
A(2x) C(2x)
H L(2x)

ACL (1)
II CH 34:7

AP (1)
II KG 23:14

APH (3)
I KG 14:23
II KG 17:9-11
II KG 18:4

APHL (2)
II CH 31:1
II CH 14:2

APL (2)
EX 34:13
DT 16:21-22

AH (3)
I KG 15:13-14
II CH 15:16-17
II CH 17:6

AHL (3)
II KG 23:4-9
II KG 23:15
JR 17:1-3
A H L(2x)

AL (7)
JG 6:25
JG 6:26
JG 6:28
JG 6:30
I KG 16:32-33
IS 17:8
IS 27:9

CP (1)
LV 26:1

CPH (none)

CPHL (none)

CPL (none)

CH (2)
PS 78:58
MI 1:3-7
C H (2x)

CHL (none)

CL (none)

PH (none)

PHL (none)

PL (4)
  EX 24:4
  IS 19:19
  HO 10:1
  HO 10:2

HL (12)
  I KG 3:4
  I KG 12:32
  II KG 18:22
  II KG 23:20
  I CH 16:39-40
  I CH 21:29
  II CH 1:3-6
    H L(2x)
  II CH 32:12
  II CH 33:15-17
    H(2x) L
  EZ 6:3-6
    H L(2x)
  EZ 6:6
  HO 10:8

Several observations about Table 2 are in order. Most striking is the long list of 12 instances of the combination HL. As found in the Hebrew Bible, this is the most frequently occurring combination of all five of the terms. The frequency of this combination is in no way surprising, especially considering the nature of the terms. The high place is the sacred location used for worship, the sanctuary area often associated with one or more particular deities. The altar is the place where offering and sacrifice are made to the deity or deities honored at the particular sanctuary. One would expect the altar and the high place to occur together frequently.

Since this study is now searching for any formulaic patterns regarding Asherah, the next observation is that in Table 2 Asherah occurs on combinations with the frequently occurring HL 3 times. Asherah occurs separately with high place 3 times and with altar a relatively frequent 7 times. Thus Table 2 reveals that Asherah occurs in combinations as found in the Hebrew Bible with high place and altar either together or separately 13 times. Why would the Asherah be found so frequently with these two other terms? Perhaps the reason is the same as that for which these two other terms are themselves found together 12 times, namely, that they all are associated with the worship of deities. Thus we find that the table bears out the assumption that the Asherah object is indeed a cultic object used along with the altar at the high place in service of deities. This, too, is not a surprising observation. What is significant about it is that it is supported by the numbers.

C. Formulas

Table 2 does not go far enough in analyzing the data since it is a simple list of the various combinations of the terms Asherah, carved image, pillar, high place, and altar exactly as they are found in the Hebrew Bible. More information is needed to make substantive conclusions. What is needed is a new table which restructures the data into a more useful form.

Table 3 is such an analysis. It is a departure from Table 2 because it no longer lists the combinations exactly as found in the Hebrew Bible. It tabulates the numerical frequency of which Asherah, carved image, pillar, high place, and altar occur with each other as they are found on Table 2.

The difference between Tables 2 and 3 can be demonstrated with the following example. From Table 2 we learn that the combination AC is not found in the Hebrew Bible in precisely that form, that is, these two terms do not occur together apart from the other three featured terms. However, these two terms can be found in combination with the other three terms. They are found with pillar (in ACP), with pillar and altar (in ACPL), and so forth. Table 3 shows that AC is found a total of 8 times within other combinations, even though they are never by themselves. Thus the first entry on Table 3 lists Asherah and carved image as being found together in the Hebrew Bible 8 times. Table 3 also is concerned with the other terms with which Asherah and carved images may be found, because it also lists the times that A and C and P are found together, and so forth.

Table 3, Numerical Frequency

Table 3 presents a simple tabulation of the numerical frequency of which A, C, P, H, and L occur with each other as they are found in Table 2. Read: A and C are found together 8 times; A, C, and P are found together 3 times, etc.

AC	8
ACP	3
ACPH	0
ACPHL	0
ACPL	2
ACH	4
ACHL	3
ACL	6
AP	11
APH	5
APHL	2
APL	6
AH	15
AHL	8
AL	20
CP	4
CPH	0
CHPL	0
CPL	2
CH	6
CHL	3
CL	6
PH	5
PHL	2
PL	8
HL	20

There are various ways to analyze the data of Table 3. The first is to note the large number of instances that certain pairs of terms are found together. Asherah and carved image are together 8 times. Asherah and pillar are together 11 times. Asherah and high place are together 15 times. Asherah and altar are together 20 times. Pillar and altar are together 8 times. High place and altar are together 20 times. What does this information suggest? First of all, it means that the hypothesis is validated that says that these terms occur together frequently. They obviously do. Since they are so often found together, one is led to call this a pattern. It is a pattern of frequent occurrence.

It is from patterns that formulas emerge. Can these particular patterns be described as formulas? No, not until they are further described. They are only a pattern of frequency, untested by any other means. They need to be further described in the contexts and literary sources of the passages in question.

The shape of the patterns begins to emerge when the largest numbers of Table 3 are compared. Asherah is found with high place 15 times and with altar 20 times. High place and altar are found together 20 times. Thus what was discovered in Table 2, that the Asherah object was frequently associated with worship at the high place and at altars, is further magnified. The numbers here are even larger than on Table 2. But are all three of these terms ever used together in the same passage? According to Table 3, they are used 8 times. This combination is a pattern of its own, whose shape can be determined by looking at its contexts.

The AHL pattern from the five cultic terms can be considered a formula. This is not only because of its frequent appearance in the Herew Bible, but more so because of the harmony of its contexts (II Kg 21:3-7, II Kg 23:4-9, II Kg 23:15, II Ch 14:2, II Ch 31:1, II Ch 33:3-7, II Ch 34:3-5, and Jr 17:1-3) which give it shape. These eight instances are all focused on one particular theme: cultic aberration. In II Kg 21:3-7 and II Ch 33:3-7 the text is critical of Manasseh who, in opposition to the deuteronomic standards, had re-incorporated these aberrations into Israelite worship. The remaining texts, except Jeremiah, are about the reformers who, in accord with the deuteronomic law code which governed the sympathies of the writers of these texts, systematically destroyed the sites and objects of foreign cult worship. The Jeremiah text is a prophetic word against the cultic aberrations which he called "the sin of Judah," the use of foreign cultic objects in the high places.

Thus a formula is identified. AHL is a cultic aberration formula. It has been demonstrated by its common theme, and it can be verified by its use, occurring 8 times in the Hebrew Bible. It is fhe first of 9 such formulaic combinations which can be identified and similarly defended.

The second formula to arise from Table 3 is a product of the combination of the terms Asherah, pillar, and altar. A and P are found together 11 times. A and L, as was noted in the first formula, are found together 20 times. P and L are found together 8 times. The resulting triad of the terms A, P, and L is found in the Hebrew Bible 6 times.

The locations of the 6 APL texts are Ex 34:13, Dt 7:5, Dt 12:3, Dt 16:21-22, II Ch 14:2, and II Ch 31:1. The Exodus passage comes from the J material which originated in the southern kingdom in the 9th or 8th century B.C.E. It is an amalgamation of J's reformulation and the deuteronomist's redaction of the E Decalogue that is found in Exodus 20.[22] Since this period of the southern monarchic history was heavily laden with cultic abuses, as II Kings and II Chronicles testify, one would expect to find this and the other strong injunctions against syncretism and apostasy within the Exodus textual account of this period. All the more so would one expect this because of the known biases of the deuteronomistic editor.

The deuteronomic texts contain similar injunctions, although they come from the Josian period of deuteronomic reforms. Both of the texts from II Chronicles are from the post-exilic period in sympathy with the deuteronomic reforms; however, they describe incidents which took place in the pre-exilic monarchical period. II Ch 14:2 speaks of the Asherah, the pillar, and the altar as cultic aberrations which had been introduced during the reigns of Solomon and his son Rehoboam. Now they were being removed by Asa, the reformer. II Ch 31:1 speaks harshly of the aberrations encouraged by Ahaz and indicates that the Asherah, the pillar, and the altar were removed in the reform movement of Hezekiah.

The terms of the second formulaic combination, Asherah, pillar, and altar, were found used together 6 times, each time in reference to cultic aberrations which spanned the period from Solomon to Hezekiah, 970 to 687 B.C.E. It is a description of a long-standing abuse, the intergration of the Asherah, the pillar, and the foreign altar into the worship of Yahweh.

Formula three is derived from the terms Asherah, pillar, and high place. These terms are found paired with each other on Table 3 as follows: A and H 15 times, A and P 11 times, and P and H 5 times. All three are used together a total of 5 times in the Hebrew Bible.

The high place was the cultic location where one might expect to find a pillar, representing the male deity, Baal, and the Asherah-post representing the female deity, Asherah. The 5 texts are I Kings 14:23, II Kg 17:9-11, II Kg 18:4, plus the two texts from II Chronicles mentioned in the description of the second formula, II Ch 14:2 and II Ch 31:1. The latter two texts are descriptions of the removal of foreign cult by the reformers. One of the the former 3 texts is also a declaration of the removal of the Asherah, the pillar, and the high place. Hezekiah (716-687) "removed the high places, shattered the pillars, and cut down the sacred poles [Asherahs]" (II Kg 18:4). The remaining two texts, in typical deuteronomistic fashion, lament the establishment of foreign cult practices among the chosen people. I Kg 14:23 castigates Judah, which under Rehoboam (930-913) allowed syncretism to run rampant. II Kg 17:9-11 castigates Israel, which under Hoshea, the last king of the northern kingdom (732-724), built numerous high places for the worship of foreign deities and "set up pillars and sacred poles [Asherahs] for themselves on every high hill and under every leafy tree" (II Kg 17:10).

This third formulaic combination, Asherah, pillar, and high place, is used 5 times in the deuteronomic texts which describe a period from 970 to 687 in both Judah and Israel. The formula is, as were the first two, a cultic aberration formula used to recall the syncretistic practices of the chosen people as they imitated their Canaanite neighbors. The terms are used not only in texts which disparage the people for their cultic aberrations, but also in texts which hail the reformers for removing the aberrations.

The fourth formula rises from the three terms Asherah, carved image, and high place. A and C are found paired 8 times. A and H are found paired 15 times. C and H are found paired in the Hebrew Bible, as found on Table 3, 6 times. All three terms are found together a total of 4 times in the Hebrew Bible.

The 4 texts where Asherah, carved image, and high place occur are II Kg 21:3-7, II Ch 33:3-7, II Ch 33:19, and II Ch 34:3-5. All but one of these texts were identified as associated with the first formula. II Kg 21:3-7 and II Ch 33:3-7 recall Manasseh rebuilding the cultic aberrations. II Ch 34:3-5 recalls Josiah destroying them. The remaining verse, II Ch 33:19, like the first two, features Manasseh in a summary recollection of his sin of erecting Canaanite cult places and objects.

The fourth formulaic combination contains Asherah, carved image, and high place. Unlike the previous three, this formula spans only a short time of history, the reign of Manasseh through the reign of Josiah, 687 through 609 in the kingdom of Judah, after the dissolution of the northern kingdom. It is a formula of cultic aberration used 3 times to recall Manasseh's cultic sins, once to credit Josiah with their removal, and in all 4 instances to criticize the presence of the Asherahs, carved images, and high places in Judah.

Another formula, the fifth one, comes from the terms Asherah, carved image, and pillar. A and C are used together 8 times. A and P are used together 11 times. C and P are used together 4 times. All three terms occur in the same passage of the Hebrew Bible 3 times.

The 3 texts where Asherah, carved image, and pillar are found together are Dt 7:5, Dt 12:3, and Mi 5:12-13. Immediately after Deuteronomy's version of the Decalogue (chapter 5) and the Shema (chapter 6), there follows an adjuration that the people should deal harshly with the Canaanite religion of the region. After being told not to enter into covenant with them and not to intermarry, in 7:5 they are instructed to destroy the sanctuaries of the Canaanites. One may assume that these commands reflect the well-founded fear that the people were all too ready to adopt Canaanite ways, and that the condoned method of reducing this foreign threat was to hamper Canaanite religious practice by destroying the Asherahs, carved images, pillars, etc. This command is consonant with the tenor of the deuteronomic reform movement which under Josiah was strongly directed toward the eradication of foreign influence in Israelite religion, an attempt to return the people to their original covenantal posture. The location of this text, so near to the text of the Shema, shows forcefully the centrality in deuteronomic reform of the purging of overtly foreign elements from Israelite religious practice.[23]

The second deuteronomic text, 12:3, occurs at the very beginning of 16 chapters of legal exposition. The command is reiterated here in nearly identical form to the commandment found in 7:5. Its occurrence in such a prominent place as the first element in the exposition of the law reaffirms its importance to the Deuteronomist. There was nothing he wanted to abolish more than these foreign practices, and his first step and most central action for accomplishing this was to call the people to destroy these cult objects, the Asherah, the carved images, and the pillars. This reveals not only the great threat they posed, but also the central role these objects must have played in the worship of the Canaanite cults. The constant and firm commands to destroy these particular things may mean that they were, in the mind of the deuteronomist, the focal points of the Canaanite worship that was keeping Israel away from its strict monotheism.

The third text is from Mi 5:12-13. Before Assyria swept through Palestine, the prophets had warned that they were coming. The people were so evil, they said, that God's punishment of allowing them to be devastated by the Assyrians was inevitable. Micah was among those hurling harsh criticism at the people for their religious corruptions and moral bankruptcy.[24] In triumphant speech about the returning glory of Judah, the Lord proclaims through Micah the destruction of all that has tended to distract the people from their God, especially foreign religious practices. Our text is a list of the three objects which Micah found particularly offensive: the Asherahs, the carved images, and the pillars. These would be abolished and removed by the Lord in the messianic age.

Thus there is the fifth formulaic combination, the Asherah, the carved image, and the pillar. Used with heightened importance by the prophet Micah and the Deuteronomist, it is an expression of the cultic aberrations whose removal from the midst of Judah were imperative.

The terms Asherah, carved image, and altar give rise to the sixth formula. A and C are found together 8 times. A and L are found 20 times. C and L are found together 6 times. The combination of A, C, and L is used a total of 6 times in the Hebrew Bible.

The 6 texts where Asherah, carved image, and altar are used together in the Hebrew Bible, according to Table 3, are Dt 7:5, Dt 12:3, II Kg 21:3-7, II Ch 33:3-7, II Ch 34:3-5, and II Ch 34:7. The first two of these texts were examined in the course of describing the fifth formula and were found to be strong and emphatic legal statements by the Deuteronomist requiring the eradication of the Canaanite cult. The next three texts were similarly examined with the first formula. In II Kg 21:3-7 the deuteronomist and in II Ch 33:3-7 the Chronicler speak critically of the reign of Manasseh (early 7th century B.C.E.) who not only permitted but fostered foreign cultic practices among the chosen people in Judah. He even erected a foreign altar in the Temple, where he also placed an Asherah-idol (21:7). In II Ch 34:3-5 the Chronicler, in sympathy with deuteronomic reform, recalls the reforms of Josiah who banned the cultic practices that had been sanctioned by Manasseh.

It is interesting that in the remaining text, II Ch 34:7, there is a repetition of the formulaic elements used only a few verses earlier in II Ch 34:3-5. There is no question here of the possibility of there being two traditions merged into one book and then maintained by an editor as two traditions printed back-to-back. These verses report with similar language two events which are chronologically and geographically separate. The first action of Josiah was taken in Judah and Jerusalem (verses 3-5), where he purged the land of its Canaanite cultus. Thereupon he moved his activity to the northen territories (verse 7), specifically named as Manasseh, Ephraim, Simeon, and Naphtali. This territory was the entire former northern kingdom, Israel, from its southern border adjoining Judah to its most northern territories, Naphtali. The action Josiah took in the area was the same as in Judah. He purged the entire area of its Canaanite cultus, specifically of its Asherahs, carved images, and foreign altars.

In the sixth formulaic combination are the terms Asherah, carved image, and altar. This formula was used by the deuteronomistic historian and by the Chronicler. They used this formula to describe the cultic aberrations which were prevalent in the worship of the chosen people and whose removal were commanded by deuteronomic law and carried out by Josiah.

A seventh formula is a result of the combining of the terms carved image, pillar, and altar. C and P are found together 4 times. C and L are found 6 times. P and L are found together 8 times. All three of these terms are found together twice in the Hebrew Bible.

The two texts where carved image, pillar, and altar occur together are Dt 7:5 and Dt 12:3. Both texts were examined for their context and content in the development of the fifth formula. They were determined to be legal statements requiring definitive action against the Canaanite cultus.

Is the seventh formulaic combination, the carved image, the pillar, and the altar, are used exclusively by the Deuteronomist as a description of the cultic aberration to be abolished.

The terms carved image, high place, and altar combine to make the eighth formula. C and H are paired 6 times in the Hebrew Bible, according to Table 3. C and L are also paired 6 times. H and L are paired 20 times. All three terms are found together 3 times in the Hebrew Bible.

The texts where the terms carved image, high place, and altar are found together are II Kg 21:3-7, II Ch 33:3-7, and II Ch 34:3-5. All three of these texts were examined in the treatment of the first formula. They were found to describe Manasseh's abuses and Josiah's correction of these abuses.

The eighth formulaic combination was used by the deuteronomic historian and the Chronicler to describe the Canaanite cultus which, according to them, was a cultic aberration.

Finally, there is the ninth formula which comes from the terms pillar, high place, and altar. P nd H are found together 5 times. P and L are found 8 times. H and L are found together 20 times. All three terms are used together twice in the Hebrew Bible.

The two texts where pillar, high place, and altar are used together in the Hebrew Bible are II Ch 14:2 and II Ch 31:1. These two texts were both noted in the descriptions of the first, second, and third formulas. They were found to be contained in critical statements about the cultic abuses engendered by Solomon, his son Rehoboam, and Ahaz.

Thus there is the ninth formulaic combination containing the terms pillar, high place, and altar. Both instances of its use by the Chronicler are descriptions of cultic aberrations found to be offensive to this post-exilic writer, who was in sympathy with the deuteronomic reform.

Modern biblical commentators have not agreed on a common meaning for the term "formula." Watters defined formula as "a repeated phrase, a distich or hemistich in length, or a repeated pair of words fixed in parallel relationship in one or more distichs of poetry."[25] If it is grounded in poetry, such a definition of formula seems out of place in the Asherah texts which are primarily narrative in character. In fact, the term "formula" is used in this study in a slightly different way. Here it means simply a recurring combination of terms.

D. The Meta-formula

It is more accurate to refer to these 9 examples as formulaic combinations rather than formulas. At least in the scientific realm, a formula is a particular combination of parts which when combined under specified conditions will always produce the same outcome. Questions of validity are easily raised when, in the instance of this study, 9 different combinations of parts have been shown to result in the nine identical outcomes, that is, 9 formulas of cultic aberration. It seems all the more questionable when the nine formulas are seen to be no more than nine re-arrangements (combinations) of the same five terms, Asherah, carved image, pillar, high place, and altar. The greatest question is generated when one compares the 9 formulas with the actual patterns or occurrences of these terms, as found on Table 2. Of the 39 times when the 9 formulas are said to occur, based on Table 3, in reality those formulas occur in their exact and exclusive manner only 11 times in the Hebrew Bible,[26] and three of the formulas are not found at all in their exact and exclusive manner.[27] The remaining 28 occurrences of the formulas are found not in an exclusive form but as part of larger combinations of terms. For example, if ACHL is found 3 times as such in the Hebrew Bible, as noted on Table 2, then 4 of the 9 formulas are found there 3 times each: ACH 3 times, ACL 3 times, AHL 3 times, and CHL 3 times.

Do these questionable data mean that the formulaic theory is undermined? While one is tempted to say yes, nevertheless there seems to be a strong attraction among the 5 terms. A glance at Table 2 shows that these terms are often used with each other in sets of 2, 3, and 4. Moreover the analysis of Table 3 showed a common deuteronomistic textual context, or at least textual sympathy with the deuteronomic reform movement, of these various terms. It also showed a common theme, the cultic aberration theme. These factors cannot be dismissed as hypothetical.

A workable solution to this problem is to change the focus. Instead of focusing on the 9 individual formulas, one should rather take a broader perspective and see all 9 formulas together. More precisely, the focus should now be placed on the 5 terms as a group rather than on the 9 formulas that are derived from them. Such a focus was not possible, however, before a study of the 9 formulaic combinations, simply because the 5 terms do not occur together in any one text of the Hebrew Bible. Therefore, it is only after looking at the parts in various forms that one can begin to speak of the conglomerated parts as being an entity in itself, a meta-formula. It is more proper to call it a meta-formula than a formula, because it is never found as such, ACPHL, in the texts. And since each of its parts is regularly found with one or more of the others, in the same context and with the same theme, it is certainly proper to call it a formulaic expression.

The meta-formula, then, is ACPHL. Its components have been shown to have been used to describe cultic aberrations throughout the monarchic periods of the united kingdom and the divided kingdoms of Judah and Israel. They are used to recall the misdeeds of kings like Solomon and Manasseh as well as the people of their kingdoms. They are also used in the context of hailing the reformers like Hezekiah and Josiah who destroyed them. They are in every instance the objects of scorn by deuteronomistic theologians who composed and edited the biblical texts. In a direct and emphatic way they are forbidden by the deuteronomic legal code where their use is outlawed and their destruction is commanded.

E. Asherah in the Meta-formula

Having suggested the use of a meta-formula which deals with the textual presentation of cultic aberrations, it is now time to return to the central element of this study, Asherah in the Hebrew Bible. What is the place of Asherah among the terms used in the meta-formula?

There are 9 formulaic combinations of the meta-formula's 5 terms. Each combination has 3 terms. Table 4 is an analysis of these 9 combinations, comparing the number of times each combination is found containing each term with the number of times it is found without. Since there are 5 terms, there are 5 comparisons.

Table 4, Asherah in the Triadic Combinations

This table compares the number of times each of the five terms found in the meta-formula is found in the 9 triadic combinations with the number of times each is absent from the 9 combinations. The number after each triad is the number of times that combination appears in the Hebrew Bible. It is the totals which are to be compared.

with Asherah		without Asherah	
AHL	8	CPL	2
APL	6	CHL	3
APH	5	PHL	2
ACH	4		7
ACP	3		
ACL	6		
	32		

with Carved Image		without Carved Image	
ACH	4	AHL	8
ACP	3	APL	6
ACL	6	APH	5
CPL	2	PHL	2
CHL	3		21
	18		

with Pillar		without Pillar	
APL	6	AHL	8
APH	5	ACH	4
ACP	3	ACL	6
CPL	2	CHL	3
PHL	2		21
	18		

with High Place	
AHL	8
APH	5
ACH	4
CHL	3
PHL	2
	22

without High Place	
APL	6
ACP	3
ACL	6
CPL	2
	17

with Altar	
AHL	8
APL	6
ACL	6
CPL	2
CHL	3
PHL	2
	27

without Altar	
APH	5
ACH	4
ACP	3
	12

Of the 39 possible times when Asherah could have been found in these combinations, Asherah was found 32 times, or 82%. This compares with 18 times (46%) for Carved Image, 18 times (46%) for Pillar, 22 times (56%) for High Place, and 27 times (69%) for Altar. It is obvious from these statistics that Asherah holds a numerically significant place in the meta-formula.

To corroborate this evidence, one can also appeal to the data in a simpler form. Table 2 lists all possible combinations of the 5 meta-formula's terms that are found in the Hebrew Bible. If one surveys these combinations, as is done in the following Table 5, a comparison can be made between the number of times each term is found and the number of times it is absent.

Table 5, Asherah and the Meta-Formula's Terms

This table compares the frequency with which each of the five terms of the meta-formula occurs within the combinations of those terms as found in he Hebrew Bible (see Table 2) with the number of times each is absent from the combinations. The number after each combination is the number of times it is found in the Hebrew Bible. The totals are to be compared.

with Asherah	
ACP	1
ACPL	2
ACH	1
ACHL	3
ACL	1
AP	1
APH	3
APHL	2
APL	2
AH	3
AHL	3
AL	7
	29

without Asherah	
CP	1
CH	2
PL	4
HL	12
	19

with Carved Image	
ACP	1
ACPL	2
ACH	1
ACHL	3
ACL	1
CP	1
CH	2
	11

without Carved Image	
AP	1
APH	3
APHL	2
APL	2
AH	3
AHL	3
AL	7
PL	4
HL	12
	37

with Pillar	
ACP	1
ACPL	2
AP	1
APH	3
APHL	2
APL	2
CP	1
PL	4
	16

without Pillar	
ACH	1
ACHL	3
ACL	1
AH	3
AHL	3
AL	7
CH	2
HL	12
	32

with High Place	
ACH	1
ACHL	3
APH	3
APHL	2
AH	3
AHL	3
CH	2
HL	12
	29

without High Place	
ACP	1
ACPL	2
ACL	1
AP	1
APL	2
AL	7
CP	1
PL	4
	19

with Altar	
ACPL	2
ACHL	3
ACL	1
APHL	2
APL	2
AHL	3
AL	7
PL	4
HL	12
	36

without Altar	
ACP	1
ACH	1
AP	1
APH	3
AH	3
CP	1
CH	2
	12

Of the 48 possible times when Asherah could have been found in these combinations, it was found 29 times or 60%. This compares with 11 times (23%) for Carved Image, 16 times (33%) for Pillar, 29 times (60%) for High Place, and 36 times (75%) for Altar. The percentage for Asherah in this table is not as high as it was in Table 4, nor is it the largest percentage on the table (75% for Altar is higher). Yet it is still high enough to be noticed as playing a dominant role in the meta-formula.

What does it mean that the Asherah term is used in a significantly high percentage of the occurrences of the terms of the meta-formula? To answer the question one must recall that the meta-formula deals with cultic aberration. If Asherah is a frequent member of these expressions denoting cultic aberrations, it could possibly be interpreted that this frequency is a reflection of the extent to which the Asherah-aberration was in use in ancient Israel and Judah. In other words, it could mean that the Asherah is not only firmly established as a dimension of the cult of ancient Israel and Judah, but also that it occurred widely, as suggested by the statement found in I Kg 14:23: "They, too, built for themselves high places, pillars, and Asherahs upon every high hill and under every green tree." At a later period, certainly by the time of the deuteronomist(s), this aspect of the cult was judged to be aberrant.

4. Conclusion

Three scholars have contributed substantially, before the 1980's, to an understanding of Asherah. Reed's study of the verbs and nouns used with Asherah substantiated the argument that Asherah in the Hebrew Bible was both a goddess and a cult object which represented her. Yamashita placed all the Asherah texts in the deuteronomistic context. Perlman contributed the idea that the word" Asherah" might be part of a formulaic expression. Although her arguments were flawed, nevertheless, her idea inspired a tabular study.

The tabular analysis assembled the data necessary to confirm a textual relationship between the terms Asherah, carved image, pillar, high place, and altar. It was determined that these terms appear with each other frequently in nine combinations. It was observed that these five terms are not found together in the same text. It is therefore more proper to call these terms members of a meta-formula rather than members of a formula, since each of its parts is found with one or more of the others regularly in the same context and with the same theme. This meta-formula was used by the biblical authors to describe cultic aberrations found in Judah and Israel during the period of the monarchy, including the worship of Asherah. The frequency of Asherah in the meta-formula's occurrences shows that among the five aberration terms of the meta-formula, Asherah is numerically the most significant. Asherah is found more often than the other terms. This suggests that Asherah worship was widely practiced in Israel and Judah.

Notes

1 All references are to the Hebrew Bible unless otherwise noted.

2 J. C. de Moor, "Asherah," in *Theological Dictionary of the Old Testament*, eds. G. Johannes Botterweck and Helmer Ringgren, vol. 1, trans. John T. Willis (Grand Rapids: William B. Eerdmans, 1979), p. 439.

3 William L. Reed, *The Asherah in the Old Testament* (Fort Worth: Texas Christian University, 1949).

4 Reed, *The Asherah*, p. 11.

5 Max Ohnefalsch-Richter, *Kypros, die Bibel und Homer* (Berlin: A. Asher and Co., 1893). Other scholars in this group are Stanley A. Cook, *The Religion of Ancient Palestine in the Light of Archaeology*, Schweich Lectures of 1925 (London: Oxford University Press, 1930); Alfred Jeremias, *The Old Testament in the Light of the Ancient East*, trans. C. L. Beaumont (London: Williams and Norgate, 1911); and Joseph Plessis, *Etude sur les textes concernant Istar-Astarte*, (Paris: Paul Geuthner, 1921).

6 This mitigation applies to all scholarship before the discovery of ancient Ugarit.

7 Karl Budde, "The Ashera in the Old Testament," *The New World* 8 (1899): 732; W. Robertson Smith, *The Religion of the Semites*, 3rd edition (London: Black, 1927).

8 G. W. Collins, "Ashtoreth and the Ashera," *The Proceedings of the Society of Biblical Archaeology* 10 (1889); A. Kuenen, *The Religion of Israel to the Fall of the Jewish State*, trans. Alfred H. May (London: Williams and Norgate, 1882).

9 For further information on early Asherah studies, see Reed, *The Asherah*, pp. 11-28.

10 Reed, *The Asherah*, pp. 29-37.

11 Reed, *The Asherah*, pp. 38-58.

12 Since Reed's biblical citations are so numerous, only two examples are given here. The reader should consult Reed for a full account.

13 Reed, *The Asherah*, pp. 55-56.

14 Reed, *The Asherah*, pp. 59-68.

15 Another text, I Kg 14:15, would place Asherah even earlier, but the date of this text is disputed. All apparently earlier texts are either later additions or are at least disputed.

16 Tadanori Yamashita, *The Goddess Asherah*, a dissertation for Yale University (Ann Arbor: University Microfilms International, 1964).

17 Yamashita, *The Goddess*, pp. 123-137.

18 Martin Noth, *Überlieferungsgeschichtliche Studien I* (Tübingen: M. Niemeyer, 1957): sect. 12f; Alexander Rofe, "The Strata of the Law About the Centralization of Worship in Deuteronomy and the History of the Deuteronomic Movement," *Vetus Testamentum* 22 (1972): 221-226.

19 Alice Lenore Perlman, *Asherah and Astarte in the Old Testament and Ugaritic Literature*, a dissertation for the Graduate Theological Union at Berkeley (Ann Arbor: University Microfilms International, 1979), pp. 6-38.

20 Perlman, *Asherah and Astarte*, p. 13.

21 Perlman, *Asherah and Astarte*, p. 11ff.

22 Otto Eissfeldt. *The Old Testament, An Introduction*, trans. P. R. Ackroyd (New York: Harper & Row, 1965), pp. 200-203; Brevard S. Childs, *The Book of Exodus; A Critical Theological Commentary* (Philadelphia: Westminster Press, 1974), pp. 601-613.

23 One must say "overtly" because many Canaanite elements such as sacrifice and various prayers were adapted by the Israelites and became acceptable practices. The purge was directed toward those elements which could not be adapted to deuteronomistic Yahwism, e.g., worship of Asherah.

24 His words were later taken up by Hezekiah who effected one of the most important reform movements of Judah's history (Jer 26:17f).

25 William R. Watters, *Formula Criticism and the Poetry of the Old Testament* (New York: Walter de Gruyter, 1976), p. 44.

26 AHL occurs three times, APL twice, APH three times, ACH once, ACP once, and ACL once.

27 CPL, CHL, and PHL are not found at all.

Chapter 4

Exodus, Deuteronomy, and Judges

1. The Exodus Text

The biblical texts from books of Exodus, Deuteronomy, and Judges which mention Asherah are placed together in one chapter only to avoid creating a multitude of small chapters. The texts appear in the order they are found in the Hebrew Bible.

The book of Exodus mentions Asherah only once. An examination of this text will reveal that it is a deuteronomistic redaction. Hence, a literary examination of the Book of Exodus is not necessary.

A. Exodus 34:13

> Tear down their altars; smash their sacred pillars, and cut down their sacred poles ['asheraw].[1]

In Exodus 34:11 the Lord has named the nations which Israel will conquer. In verse 12 he forbids Israel to make a covenant with any of them. Now, in verse 13, the Lord commands Israel to destroy the cult objects of the nations. Among these objects are the Asherahs.

There is controversy regarding the literary origin of this text. Perlman[2] discussed this debate, maintaining some regard for placement of the text in the J tradition. She suggested that because the Asherah was not known or recorded in Israel's early history, i.e., before entering Canaan, then they must have first learned about Asherah when they entered Canaan. If this is true, she says, then one can date this text after the settlement and before

Deuteronomy. Perlman does not consider, however, that the Asherah, who was known in Canaan before the Israelites, fleeing from Egypt to Canaan, had learned of her, must have been known to the ancestors of the Israelites who had never left Canaan. Therefore, it is possible, from a historical perspective, that the text pre-dates the settlement.

Nevertheless, considering the later date of the composition of Exodus, it is still impossible to be certain of an early origin. This text's lack of unity with its context allows a considerable latitude of probabilities for its time of origin in Israelite history, and ought to be considered a deuteronomistic redaction until proved otherwise.

Another matter to consider is the close similarity of this text to Dt 7:5. Given this similarity, it is difficult to say that they are unrelated. It is much easier to suggest that Ex 34:13 is a deuteronomistic addition to the text of Exodus.[3] Many scholars are in agreement with the position that this is a deuteronomistic addition.[4]

Reed[5] described this passage as a late redaction and agreed that, because of its similarity to the Dt passage, it was probably the work of the later editor who shaped the Exodus text to resemble the more familiar deuteronomic version of the law. He also noted that this supposition denies the text any possibility of being used to show that Moses knew Asherah, a loss which he does not mourn.

Childs engaged in a fuller study of the literary origin of the Exodus texts.[6] He attributed most of chapter 14 to a pre-deuteronomic redactor who was combining the J and E strands. However he saw 11-13 and 15-16 as a deuteronomistic expansion of this redaction. He called it a homiletic introduction to the covenant stipulations, emphasizing Israel's complete separation from its neighbors.

The verse begins with the *ki*, a conjunction which gives this verse an emphatic connection to the previous verse. Perlman[7] pointed out that this shows that verse 13 is a command which, if carried out, will prevent Israel from becoming involved with the cults of the nations residing in the promised land. Thus Israel will avoid suffering the consequences of this involvement as described in verses 15-16.

The term "altar" is not identified here beyond its identity as a foreign cult object. Reed[8] observed that one can assume sacrifice and some association with a particular local deity. In the eight verses where it is linked to a deity, that deity is always Baal.[9] Vaughan[10] gave some assistance in translating this term. He notes that the LXX translates *mizbēah* with two theologically distinct words: *bōmos*, meaning the altar of a foreign deity, and *thysiastērion*, meaning a Yahwist altar.

> However, while *bōmos* can be used interchangeably with *thysiastērion* for the Temple altar, the reverse is not the case. *Thysiastērion* is never used of pagan altars. In other words, at all times *bōmos* retained its character as the natural word used for pagan altars.[11]

Interestingly, *bōmos* is also used to translate *bāmā* in several instances, including the present passage, suggesting that there may have been some kind of conscious association between the altar and the high place, or at least their common use in the foreign cult. Alternatively, the Greek translator may simply have been transliterating the Hebrew.

This passage uses the term "pillars" with Asherah. To help discover the significance of this pairing of terms, Reed[12] discussed the pillars, which were columns of stone.[13] It is easy to suggest that these were similar in nature and function to the Asherah posts; however, the text does not allow such a specific comparison. Reed observed that these two terms are used together only 11 times[14], and in each of these instances they are named along with other cult objects and not necessarily as a pair. Reed did note, however, that there is another way of looking at the text. While it is possible that the terms were similar, the texts do not show it. This, however, does not deny the possibility of their being similar. The texts merely refrain from affirming it or other possibilities.

There was a relationship between Asherah and pillar. De Moor[15] noted that in I Kg 3:2 and 10:26-27 the pillar is specifically associated with Baal, and that the post is associated by name with

Asherah. This would be a natural association of the deities, who governed fertility and nurturing respectively.

The verb *kārat* is used with Asherah. Reed[16] noted that this word has a special meaning when used in covenantal texts, e.g., Gn 15:18, Ex 34:27. Yet he is able to distinguish this use from its present context, which much more closely resembles other texts in which it is used to describe the cutting down of a tree, e.g., Dt 19:5, Is 44:14, Jr 10:3. It is a word used to indicate the action of severing and toppling an upright object made of wood. A plain pole or a carved one would do nicely, as would a living tree, to explain what is meant by the Asherah in Ex 34:13. Reed did not prove which of these is indicated, though he clearly favors the pole over the living tree.

Ugaritic parallels to any of the 40 Asherah verses are rare. There is RS 17.227 which shows similarities in content to Ex 34:10-26. It is a covenant between Niqmadu, King of Ugarit and Suppiluliuma, King of Hatti. It does not contain any direct parallel to Exodus 34:13.

Thus Ex 34:13, a deuteronomistic redaction, shows that Asherah is associated with the altar, a foreign cult place of sacrifice, and the pillar, which was a stone pillar used in the worship of Baal. If the Asherah is a wooden post, as is indicated by the verb *kārat*, then the pillar used with it would seem to associate the deities they represent, Asherah and Baal.

2. The Texts of Deuteronomy

The outlook of the book of Deuteronomy is from the 7th century, from the viewpoint of the Josian reform. There are only three texts in the book of Deuteronomy which mention Asherah. An examination of these texts will reveal the deuteronomic writer's harsh criticism of the widespread worship of Asherah. There will be a discussion of the term "carved image" which has been important in this study. Asherah will be clearly identified as both a female deity and a cult object. This cult object, called an Asherah, is a wooden post. Furthermore, it will be demonstrated that an Asherah had been constructed in the Temple of Yahweh.

There is an interesting theory for understanding the editing of Deuteronomy. De Tillesse[17] observed that after having removed all the plural passages, the remainder of singular passages form a coherent whole. He also noted that the body of plural passages are notably similar to the deuteronomistic books of Joshua through Kings both in style and theology. Two of the texts, Dt 7:5 and 12:3, are among the plural texts which are indeed reflected in the later deuteronomistic books. The third Asherah text, Dt 16:21, is a singular text.

A. Deuteronomy 7:5

> But this is how you must deal with them: Tear down their altars, smash their sacred pillars, chop down their sacred poles [wa'ăshêrēhem], and destroy their idols by fire.

Although the order is different, the terms used in this verse are similar to those in Ex 34:10-16. Perlman pointed out, however, that the use of fire for the destruction of idols (*wûp*^{e}*sîlêhem*) is unique to the book of Deuteronomy.[18] One wonders from what materials they might have been constructed. In this verse they were ordered to be burned, and in 12:3 shattered. Perhaps the solution is to suggest that they were not all alike, that there were various kinds of idols, some of which could be burned, some shattered, etc. If this were the case, then it would be possible to include a wooden Asherah in the category of idols along with stone pillars, metal and clay figurines, etc.

This text appears in a longer passage which is a cultic regulatory sermon. Von Rad[19] described this text and its context, verses 1-26, as a sermon whose purpose is to regulate the future relationship of Israel to its new Canaanite neighbors. He noted that its theology, being later than the event itself, has a much more radical view of separatism than the Israel of earlier times. Although von Rad was not so explicit, one might expect that things such as intermarriage (Rachel the Aramaean) and the use of pillars and Asherah in worship, all of which were prohibited in the deuteronomic era, were practiced rather freely in the early days of Israel.

Blenkinsopp noted that even in the later monarchy, the reform movements were implemented only sporadically. After the settlement and in every century of the monarchy, many Canaanite altars and sanctuaries continued to function. He described the pillar as "a baalist and phallic symbol" and the Asherah as "the equivalent for the goddess of the same name, consort of El in the Ugaritic texts and of Baal in the Old Testament."[20]

The term "carved image" plays an important role in this study. Reed discussed *pesel*, the idol or carved image. He said that the term was used to describe images made for deities, but that the word is never associated with particular deities in the Hebrew Bible. He observed, "They were doubtless made for all the deities."[21] He noted that the mention of both 'Asherah' and 'idol' together need not lead one to conclude that they are mutually exclusive. On the contrary, he pointed to I Kg 21:7 which associates the two with each other. Thus, as was noted above, it is all the more probable that the Asherah was one of many kinds of idols.

The carved image and the Asherah are shown by this verse to be related. De Moor[22] further explained the appearance together of Asherah and idol in this verse. He said that the Asherah is perhaps given specific mention because she was the most important female deity. If any idol would have been singled out, it would have been the one for the goddess Asherah. De Moor also noted that the Asherah, an object made of wood, and the pillar, an object made of stone, are found together very often. This is a noteworthy observation. Israel's ancient sanctuaries often contained both wood and stone (Joshua 24:26, Gn 35:8, Jg 6:11, etc.). These ancient wooden forms could have preceded knowledge of Asherah in Israel, in which case the Asherah in the present text would have been a later specification of the deity, Asherah. If Asherah was not known in those earlier sanctuaries, then the Asherah wood in the present text could be said to have taken over the role of the ancient unspecified wood among the cultic objects. De Moor also noted that stone and wood were combined in ancient Ugarit. They were worshiped and they played a role in giving oracles.

Ringgren took up the matter of the pillars.

> The Asherah represented the female divinity; the massebah beside it served as a symbol of the presence of the male god. These stones were smeared with blood or fat, moistened with drink offering, or kissed by the worshiper. Excavations have unearthed several such massebahs. The Greeks saw them in Phoenicia and Syria and gave them the name *baitulos* or *baitulion*, a word that retains a reminiscence of the term bêt'ēl, "house of God".[23]

After noting that some of the ancient stories of Israel involve trees in a special way (Gn 12:6, 13:18, 21:33; Jg 9:37; etc.), he cautioned that

> Only one thing can be said with assurance: sacred stones and sacred trees played a part in the religion of that period. It is quite possible, however, that details of the stories in question reflect conditions of a much later period.[24]

The verb "to chop down" gives a clue to the identity of the Asherah and the idols. Reed[25] made mention of *gada'* in a brief fashion. The LXX translates both this and *kārat* (from Ex 34:13) with *ἐkkópsete*, that is "to cut off." It is noteworthy that in this text it is used to describe what was done to the Asherahs, the wood, and also in 12:3 to describe what was done to the idols. One might suppose that at least some of the idols in question might also be wooden.

B. Deuteronomy 12:3

> Tear down their altars, smash their sacred pillars, destroy by fire their sacred poles [wa'ăshêrēhem], and shatter the idols of their gods, that you may stamp out the remembrance of them in any such place.

This text stands at the very head of the great legal section of Deuteronomy, delineated by von Rad[26] as 12:2 - 26:15. As is obvious, the first concern of this law is the centralization of the cult. Von Rad referred especially to 13:2-4, where there is the implication that foreign cults were alive and vital in the midst of Israel. It is because of this vitality of the foreign cults that there arose the strong adjurations to stamp them out and rid the land of them.

This legal section may be longer than von Rad suggested. Blenkinsopp[27] extended the great legal section farther than von Rad, including 12:1 at the beginning, and describing the end as 28:68. He showed that chapter 12 is a conflation of two, perhaps even three versions of the law.

Perlman[28] focused on the first verses, showing that the general deuteronomic intent to centralize the cult is exemplified here. Verse 2 commands the elimination of the foreign cult objects. Although Perlman did not say so, one might presume that the cult objects were found at those sanctuaries and perhaps elsewhere, too. If so, the presence of Asherah in these sanctuaries was widespread.

In verse 2 there is reference to the leafy trees. This is interesting when contrasted with verse 3. If, as de Moor[29] suggested, the wood was the cult object which was the forerunner of Asherah worship, then the fact that it is mentioned here, separate and apart from Asherah, suggests that it had evolved to such a point that the Asherah was no longer associated with the live tree or the groves, *ålsos*, as the LXX so often translated Asherah. Asherah was now associated exclusively with the dead wooden pole erected in the sanctuary, perhaps carved or stylized in some way.

Before continuing, it should be noted that there was some confusion in the Hebrew Bible regarding the identity of the foreign female deity worshiped by the Israelites. Gibson[30] suggested that there is a passage in the Ugaritic texts of the Baal cycle (3, C, lines 18-20) which contains a cultic nuance. The text speaks in a cryptic way to what may be a reference to important cult objects, pillars of stone and wooden posts or trees.

dm.rgm i̓ṯ.ly.w.a̓rgmk
hwt.w.aṯnyk
rgm ᶜs.w.lḫšt.a̓bn

For I have a tale that I would tell you,
a word that I would repeat to you,
a tale of tree(s) and a whisper of stone(s)...

In this story the characters involved are Baal and his consort Anat, rather than Baal and Asherah. Gibson's suggestion has merit, nevertheless, because in the Hebrew Bible the goddess Anat is not mentioned, but Asherah and Baal seem to be paired by those who worshiped both (I Kg 18). This transference was apparently made by the time of the writing of the Hebrew Bible, perhaps earlier, even by the time of the early prophets.

C. Deuteronomy 16:21

> 21You shall not plant a sacred pole ['ăšhērāh] of any kind of wood beside the altar of the lord, your God, which you will build; 22nor shall you erect a sacred pillar, such as the Lord, your God detests.

This text differs from Dt 7:5 and 12:3. Note that it does not command the destruction of Asherah as did the other Dt texts, but rather now it forbids their construction. This prohibition applies to practices within the Temple. What is implied by this verse is not only that Israel wanted to build Asherahs in the Temple, but also that they probably already had. Reed[31] agreed that this implies the construction of Asherah in conjunction with the Temple, therefore, with the Yahwistic altars. He noted that altars and Asherahs are both of Canaanite origin, and asked legitimately why the former were mandated in the law and the latter forbidden. His answer was that the Asherah retained the identity of the Canaanite religion while the altar did not.

Implicit in Reed's answer is a further answer. The altar became associated with Yahweh and was adapted to Yahwistic practices. Yahweh had, in Israelite religion, taken over the place of El and Baal in Canaanite religion. Asherah, on the other hand, could not be replaced by anyone from the Israelite religion, because there was no female Israelite deity to take her place. Therefore, she retained her own identity, the goddess Asherah, now a common and familiar part of Israelite religion. This suggestion clarifies the reason for the prohibition against constructing Asherahs. They were a real threat to deuteronomistic Yahwism.

Reed also said that one must not construe Asherah worship as merely a late manifestation of the ancient Israelite association of Yahweh worship and trees (cf. Gn 13:18), for if the Israelites had intended such, there would be little reason for the deuteronomist to object. On the contrary, the Asherah must be construed as having been separate from the ancient image of the tree.[32] The Asherah was a wooden object dedicated to a specific deity, the goddess Asherah, an object which was to be "planted" next to the altar of Yahweh.

Since Asherah was, as a cult object, associated with the altar, a Yahwist cult object, a further argument arises. If the Israelites understood a living deity to be present at the Yahwist cult object, i.e., Yahweh at the altar, then they very probably understood another living deity, Asherah, to be present at the Asherah object, the wooden pole. Of course this object was forbidden by the law, but it seems that they were not inhibited by such regulation. Otherwise there would be no need for such an aggressive prohibition as is found in this text of Deuteronomy. Asherah was worshiped right alongside of Yahweh in the Temple. Asherah worship was, therefore, a common part of popular Israelite religion.

Von Rad agreed that the Asherah was a cultic wooden pole which penetrated Yahwism from the Canaanite fertility cults. It was regarded as inappropriate by the conservatives. He also stated that because of "the prohibition of Asherim and Masseboth beside the altar of Yahweh," which "presupposes a number of sanctuaries and not the centralization of the cult," one might suppose that this tradition "must have come from the pre-Deuteronomic period."[33] This statement is difficult to understand, since Asherah and altar appear in the singular in this verse, not in the plural. Von Rad's comment would be more valid if it were applied to 7:5 and 12:3. Nevertheless, because of 7:5 and 12:3, his conclusion is correct that the cult was widespread and existed before Deuteronomy.

A further comment is possible about the relationship between Yahweh and Asherah. Reed[34] suggested that the cultic ties between Yahweh and Asherah were such that the people of Israel were naturally led to see them in relation to one another. Yamashita[35] went further and said that the Israelites attempted to make Yahweh and Asherah a divine couple. He saw this tendency implicit in this text. Blenkinsopp agreed and said that the Asherah here refers to "a statue of the goddess as consort of Yahweh, set up in the shrine."[36]

The verb "to plant" is used with Asherah only in this text. Reed[37] discouraged any attempts to suggest from this text that Asherah is a real, living tree, in spite of passages such as Lv 19:23 in which the verb describes the planting of live trees. Instead he said that the verb suggests that Asherah was a pole or image to be set up, and that planting is an image to describe its setting up. He cited as evidence Dn 11:45 where the verb is used to describe the pitching of a tent, and Jr 24:6, 32:31 and Ps 44:3 where it describes the establishment of persons or causing persons to dwell. Given the versatility of this verb, the narrower interpretation of "planting trees" is certainly not required.

The three texts of Deuteronomy have added considerably to an understanding of the nature of Asherah. First, they show by their importance and harshness that the worship of Asherah was a most serious problem and that the deuteronomic writer(s) saw Asherah as a threat to Yahwism. Second, they indicate that the wooden Asherah was an idol. Third, they affirm that Asherah worship in foreign cult places was widespread. Fourth, they reveal a prohibition from the deuteronomist that an Asherah post was not permitted in the Temple of Yahweh, implying that there was an Asherah post in the Temple. Fifth, the texts suggest that Asherah was present at her cult object in much the same way that Yahweh was thought to be present at his cult object, the altar. Hence the Israelites were worshiping both Yahweh and Asherah as a divine couple, as Yahweh their chief God and Asherah, his consort.

3. The Texts of Judges

Soggin[38] divided the text of Judges into three parts: first, the conquest narratives, 1:1-2:5; second, the main body, 2:6-16:31;

third, the pro-monarchic appendix, two episodes about Dan and Benjamin, 17-21. All three parts express the deuteronomic theological viewpoints, although in part three the indications of this are quite subtle. The Judges texts in this study are from part two, the main body.

There are only two passages in Judges which mention Asherah, but they are revealing. This study will show that Asherah worship was widespread and was viewed in popular Hebrew religion as consonant with and not opposed to the worship of Yahweh. The Israelites were loyal to the worship of Asherah. This section will also discuss an opposing viewpoint which suggests that the Asherah is a grove of trees.

A. Judges 3:7

> Because the Israelites had offended the Lord by forgetting the Lord, their God, and serving the Baals and Asherahs [hā'ăšhêrôth], 8the anger of the Lord flared up against them...[39]

This text is part of a story. In the beginning of the story, where our text occurs, Israel is reported as having served Baal and Asherah, a shameful act. Then, as a result of this sin, the angry God delivered them over to king Cushan-reshathaim of Mesopotamia. After eight years of foreign dominance, the Israelites begged God for mercy. God relented and sent them the judge named Othniel to save them. Othniel conquered Cushan-reshathaim and delivered Israel.

It is commonly agreed among scholars that this verse is part of an authentic judge narrative. Eissfeldt[40] considered Jg 3:7 - 16:31 as the actual judge narrative, introduced by 3:7. He said that 3:7 comes from the deuteronomistic compiler as an addition to earlier material. Richter[41] gave a more extensive explanation, but was essentially in agreement with Eissfeldt that this verse is a deuteronomistic redaction. Both Crossan and Soggin[42] also described this verse as a deuteronomistic introduction to the judge stories.

Regarding the verb *ᶜebed*, Reed[43] noted that the meaning was "to serve" or "to worship." It can be used both with deities (Jg 2:7, 2:13) or with cult objects (Dt 4:19, 8:19; II Kg 17:12). Commenting on the Asherah in this text, he said that

> the probability is that it referred to a goddess (the female companion of Baal with whom she is there mentioned). If the Asherah was also her image, then we should understand by the fact that people *served* her the practice of placing sacrifices before that object of the cult.[44]

In stating that if Asherah meant here an image, we should understand that the people placed sacrifices before the image, Reed made an assumption that has little defense. But it is an interesting and thought-provoking assumption.

Asherah and Baal appear in this verse in the plural. Reed's explanation is a simple one. He suggested that it indicates "that each locality had its Baal and its Asherah who were consorts worshiped at the same sanctuary."[45] Since the worship of Baal and Asherah was never centralized in the history of Canaan, this is a likely explanation.

The connection between Asherah and other deities similar to her in the Hebrew Bible is a complex question. Giving some background to this question, de Moor[46] noted that Asherah was the wife of El in Ugarit, but she appears in the Hebrew Bible as the consort of Baal, a role formerly held by Anat in the Ugaritic myths. De Moor explained that this change was the result of a later development, near the end of the second millennium, in which Asherah, the mother-goddess, began to be fused with Anat and Astarte, the fertility goddesses. The result of this fusion was the disappearance of Asherah's identity as mother-goddess and her assumption of the fertility role. De Moor might also have added that another result of this fusion was the beginning of the never-ending confusion of the names of the deities Asherah, Anat, and Astarte, such that their names were sometimes used interchangeably, especially Asherah and Astarte in the Hebrew Bible.

There are in the Hebrew Bible a number of rather close parallels to this text which contain Ashtaroth instead of Asherah (Jg 2:13,

3:7, 10:6; I Sam 7:4, 12:10). Reed dealt with this complication with the following:

> The burden of the author of the book of Judges was not to describe the identity and nature of the pagan deities being worshiped but to point out that the people had forsaken the worship of Yahweh.[47]

The text of 3:7 and other rather general statements like it, e.g., 10:6, suggest that the author(s) had either little interest in or knowledge of the Canaanite deities. He may have distinguished little difference between Asherah and Astarte, but by using both names he suggested two deities, both of whom were associated with Baal.

One must be cautious when considering the nature of the Hebrew worship of Asherah. Ahlström[48] pointed out that this text does not suggest that Israel actually abandoned Yahweh, in the sense of apostasy. The people of earlier epochs did not subscribe to the strict regulations of the deuteronomistic redactors. The early willingness to associate Yahweh with El is only one of many signs that Canaanite religious practices were added to Yahwism. Asherah worship may well have been viewed as consonant with Yahwism in the earlier times.

B. Judges 6:25b, 26b, 28, 30b

> 25That same night the Lord said to him, "Take the seven-year-old spare bullock and destroy your father's altar to Baal and cut down the sacred pole [hā'ăšhērāh] that is by it. 26You shall build, instead, the proper kind of altar to the Lord, your God, on top of this stronghold. Then take the spare bullock and offer it as a holocaust on the wood from the sacred pole [hā'ăšhērāh] you have cut down." 27So Gideon took ten of his servants and did as the Lord had commanded him. But through fear of his family and of the townspeople, he would not do it by day, but did it at night. 28Early the next morning the townspeople found that the altar of Baal had been destroyed, the sacred pole [wehā'ăšhērāh] near it cut down, and the spare bullock offered on the altar that was built. 29They asked one another, "Who did this?" Their inquiry led them to the conclusion that Gideon, son of Joash, had done it. 30So the townspeople said to Joash, "Bring out your son that he may die, for he has destroyed the altar of Baal and has cut down the sacred pole [hā'ăšhērāh] that was near it."

This passage suggests that Asherah worship was, in those earlier days, a communal or a public affair. Patai[49] noted that Gideon's father, Joash the Abiezrite, was the community priest of Asherah and Baal as well as the owner of the Asherah image. He also happened to be the town chieftain of Ofra. Gideon was in the poor predicament of having to defend Yahwism against the wishes of his powerful father and in conflict with the religious practice of his townspeople. In the end, Gideon was saved from death only because of the intervention of his father.

This passage is a deuteronomistic expansion. Eissfeldt[50] said, however, that this text precedes the deuteronomistic redactor. But he did admit that there is a theme in common with Deuteronomy, namely that God punishes sin with distress and rewards penitence with deliverance. On the contrary, Soggin[51] showed that Eissfeldt's statement is no longer to be regarded as accurate, that this text is actually a deuteronomistic expansion of the original story.

The names in the story are interesting. The father's name, Joash, as Albright[52] pointed out, is a Yahwist name, while the given name of Gideon, Jerubbaal, is apparently from the Baal cult. One suspects, however, that since Joash was in fact a Baalist, he apparently fell away from the Yahwist religion of his parents who gave him a Yahwist name. Crossan[53] gave a different interpretation to Gideon's name, a little kinder than Albright's. Crossan noted that the term "baal" was a general term, especially in Israel's early days. It was the Canaanite word, adopted and used by the Israelites, for "lord." Therefore one cannot assume that a "-baal" name in early Israel necessarily implied devotion to the god, Baal. On the contrary, the term was applied equally to Yahweh, the Lord, and thus a "-baal" name can easily be interpreted as an acknowledgment that Yahweh is the Lord. It was not until later that the term "baal" was associated exclusively with idolatry. At that time its use as a suffix to names died out. Crossan's observations can be taken another step. It can be said that Gideon was himself an early example of the growing disuse of the "-baal" suffix. Gideon dropped his "-baal" name and took a name more acceptable to the Yahwistic cult.

For an explanation of the nature of the "spare" bull, Boling's[54] suggestion is quite sufficient. He said that the spare bull is the one which is second in line to the first bull, while the first bull was the one kept for the development of the herd. The fact that they would preserve the first bull for the herd and use the second for sacrifice reveals domestic reform to the extent that their priorities were now in husbandry.

There is one scholar who disagreed with the more common interpretations of Asherah in this verse, and who would likely disagree with the entire premise of this study. Edward Lipinski[55] had an opinion, held by few, that Asherah in this verse (and throughout the Hebrew Bible) is not a deity or a wooden cult object, but rather is a Canaanite sacred grove of trees. To defend his position, he noted that the words "cut down" and "plant," the use of Asherah as firewood, and the use of 10 servants to cut down the Asherah are all evidence that points to the Asherah being a grove of considerable size.

This is not a position easily maintained. To begin with, Reed[56] has offered sufficient explanation of the verbs "to plant" and "to cut down" to show that they do not necessarily apply to living trees. Second, a grove of trees is not needed to sacrifice a bull. One large wooden post, cut in pieces, would be quite sufficient and perhaps superior as firewood because it would be dry. And third, Lipinski's assumption that the 10 servants were needed to cut down trees is incorrect. Gideon could easily have cut down the Asherah pole alone, but he would have needed his servants for protection against the townspeople should they catch him cutting down their beloved Asherah. It is evident from the text that the townspeople were hostile, that they wanted to kill Gideon even after the fact. Surely they would have been enraged had they caught him in the act.

This verse seems to have been troublesome to those who misunderstood the nature of the Asherah. Recently, Peter Höffken[57] described the Asherah in this verse not as a goddess, but as a cult object that is related to the Canaanite god, Baal. He dismissed Asherah, the goddess, because she had nothing to do with this passage. He was apparently unaware of the evidence.

This text may indicate that Asherah worship was practiced early in the history of the Israelites and represents a transfer of allegiance. Mendenhall and Ahlström[58] have both made interesting and helpful observations about this text. Mendenhall said that this story represents a transfer of allegiance from the local deities, Baal and Asherah, to Yahweh. This is an act of cultic significance, albeit not a permanent shift, as the future of Israel and Judah revealed. Ahlström concluded from this passage and from Jg 3:7 that Asherah was worshiped by the Israelites at least from the earliest times of entry after the Exodus.

Another of Reed's[59] suggestions is significant for this study. He said that the presence of the Asherah object beside the altar of Baal suggests that the townspeople were serving both of them at the same sanctuaries, probably as consorts. This is significant when one notes how the Asherah stood next to the altar of Yahweh in the Hebrew cult. It is likely that Asherah and Yahweh were considered consorts.

Since, as noted above, this text has been determined to be a deuteronomistic expansion, and since the only other mention of Asherah in the book of Judges is also a deuteronomistic redaction, does this suggest, then, that there was perhaps no goddess Asherah in the original story, and that the Asherah was mentioned in this text only because she was in the mind of the deuteronomist, not because she was actually worshiped by the townsfolk of Gideon? No, it should not be assumed that Asherah worship in this story was the creation of the deuteronomist, for several reasons. First, the pre-monarchic times were the heyday of Asherah worship among the Canaanites. It is inconceivable that the Israelites, who were penetrating Canaanite territories at this time, would have been unaware of Asherah. Second, it is unlikely that the Israelites, in their syncretistic adoption of Canaanite religious practices, e.g. Baal worship, would have excluded such an attractive practice as Asherah worship. Thus, while it can be said that this text, because it is a deuteronomistic redaction, cannot render a firm confirmation that Asherah worship was taking place during the time of the judges, nevertheless, the text can be said not to deny the occurrence of religious events, such as Asherah worship, which were most likely happening, despite their omission from the original form of the story.

In the books of Exodus, Deuteronomy, and Judges, Asherah was understood to be a nurturing deity when the Hebrews learned of her from the Canaanites. She had been the favorite goddess of the Canaanites from early on. Her cult object was an idol, a wooden post, which stood near the altar in the sanctuary.

The bulk of the information we have from this segment of the Hebrew Bible about Asherah comes from the deuteronomistic redactor(s), whose attitudes toward Asherah worship was decidedly and understandably negative, but who nevertheless provided substantial insights into the nature of Asherah.

Asherah was known to the Israelites both as a goddess and her cult object. The people were inclined to worship her, and this worship was widespread among them. It existed from the earliest days of settlement, from their first encounters with the Canaanites.

While the deuteronomistic redactor(s) firmly opposed the worship of Asherah, popular religion up to the time of the deuteronomist reveled in it. There is even reason to believe that Asherah was considered the consort of Yahweh. This did not represent apostasy in the people's eyes, but rather a natural joining of two neighboring religious systems, the joining of the cult of Baal and the cult of Yahweh, where Yahweh took the place of Baal as Asherah's consort.

By the middle of the first millennium B.C.E., Asherah was sometimes called Anat and Astarte. In the deuteronomistic accounts of the Hebrew Bible there is constant confusion between Asherah and Astarte. This confusion of the role of Asherah included the role of the nurturing mother-goddess and fertility-goddess, as Astarte was known to be. The three seemed to have fused in their identity. But in the early Hebrew days there was little confusion. Asherah was the goddess they worshiped.

Notes

1 Instead of *ʾăšērâw*, *ʾăšērêhem* or its equivalent is found in the Syriac, the Aramaic Targum (Sperber), the Pseudo Johathan Targum, and the Hebrew-Samaritan Pentateuch (von Gall).

2 Alice Lenore Perlman, *Asherah and Astarte in the Old Testament and Ugaritic Literatures*, dissertation for the Graduate Theological Union, Berkeley, California (Ann Arbor: University Microfilms International, 1979), pp. 26-30. John E. Huesmann, S. J., "Exodus," in *The Jerome Biblical Commentary*, eds. Raymond E. Brown, S. S., et al. (Englewood Cliffs, New Jersey: Prentice-Hall, Inc., 1968), pp. 65-6 agrees that it is the Jahwist. Otto Eissfeldt, *The Old Testament: An Introduction*, trans. P. R. Ackroyd (New York: Harper & Row, 1965), p. 193 calls it the L source, although with reservations.

3 Perlman, *Asherah and Astarte*, p. 20 observed this similarity; however, it is not easy to dismiss it as she does.

4 For a further discussion of this text as a deuteronomistic addition, see Martin Noth, *Überlieferungsgeschichtliche Studien I* (Tübingen: M. Niemeyer, 1957), section 12; A. Weiser, *Einleitung in das Alte Testament* (Gottingen: Vandedhoeck und Ruprecht, 1957), p. 149; and Norman C. Habel, *Yahweh Versus Baal: A Conflict of Religious Cultures* (New York: Bookman Associates, 1964), p. 34, nt. 35.

5 William L. Reed, *The Asherah in the Old Testament* (Fort Worth: Texas Christian University, 1949), p. 65.

6 Brevard S. Childs, *The Book of Exodus: A Critical, Theological Commentary* (Philadelphia: Westminster Press, 1974), pp. 604-613.

7 Perlman, *Asherah and Astarte*, p. 14.

8 Reed, *The Asherah*, p. 46.

9 Jg 6:25, 26, 30; I Kg 16:32; II Kg 21:3; II Ch 33:3, 34:4, and 7.

10 Patrick H. Vaughan, *The Meaning of "BAMA" in the Old Testament* (Cambridge, England: Cambridge University Press, 1974), pp. 34-5.

11 Vaughan, *BAMA*, p. 71, nt. 41.

12 Reed, *The Asherah*, pp. 48-9.

13 Huesman, "Exodus," pp. 65-6 recalls the numerous pillars unearthed at Gezer.

14 Reed did not provide citations. They are Ex 34:13; Dt 7:5, 12:3, 16:21-22; I Kg 14:23; II Kg 17:10, 23:14; I Ch 14:3, 15:16-17, 31:1; Mi 5:13-14.

15 J. C. de Moor, "Asherah," in *Theological Dictionary of the Old Testament*, Vol. 1, eds. G. Johannes Botterweck and Helmer Ringgren (Grand Rapids: William B. Eerdmans, 1979), p. 443.

16 Reed, *The Asherah*, p. 33.

17 G. Minette de Tillesse, "Sections 'tu' et sections 'vous' dans le Deuteronome," *Vetus Testamentum* 12 (1962):29-87. This theory is largely accepted by Ernest W. Nicholson, *Deuteronomy and Tradition* (Philadelphia: Fortress Press, 1967).

18 Perlman, *Asherah and Astarte*, pp. 17-19.

19 Gerhard von Rad, *Deuteronomy: A Commentary*, trans. Dorothea Barton (Philadelphia: Westminster Press, 1966), pp. 67-8.

20 Joseph Blenkinsopp, "Deuteronomy," in *The Jerome Biblical Commentary*, eds. Raymond E. Brown, S.S., et al. (Englewood Cliffs, New Jersey: Prentice-Hall, Inc., 1968), p. 107.

21 Reed, *The Asherah*, p. 49.

22 De Moor, "Asherah," pp. 440, 443.

23 Helmer Ringgren, *Israelite Religion*, trans. David E. Green (Philadelphia: Fortress Press, 1975), p. 24.

24 Ringgren, *Israelite Religion*, p. 26.

25 Reed, *The Asherah*, pp. 33-4.

26 Von Rad, *Deuteronomy*, pp. 89, 92.

27 Blenkinsopp, in *JBC*, p. 110.

28 Perlman, *Asherah and Astarte*, pp. 19-20.

29 As above, under Dt 7:5.

30 J. C. L. Gibson, *Canaanite Myths and Legends*, 2nd. ed. (Edinburgh: T. & T. Clark, 1978), p. 49, nt. 4.

31 Reed, *The Asherah*, pp. 41-2.

32 G. W. Ahlström, *Aspects of Syncretism in Israelite Religion* (Lund: C. W. K. Gleerup, 1963), pp. 50-51 agrees that this was no tree, but a cult object, and that Asherah was both a cult object and the proper name of a deity.

33 Von Rad, *Deuteronomy*, p. 115.

34 Reed, *The Asherah*, p. 88.

35 Tadanori Yamashita, *The Goddess Asherah*, a dissertation for Yale University (Ann Arbor: University Microfilms Internationl, 1964), p. 127.

36 Blenkinsopp, in *JBC*, p. 112.

37 Reed, *The Asherah*, p. 32.

38 Alberto J. Soggin, *Judges: A Commentary* (Philadelphia: Westminster Press, 1981), pp. 4-5.

39 According to two Hebrew Mss, the Vulgate, and the Syriac texts, *ha as^{e}ttarot* is suggested.

40 Eissfeldt, *The OT*, pp. 243, 258.

41 W. Richter, "Zu den Richtern Israels," *Zeitschrift für die Alttestamentliche Wissenschaft* 77 (1965):40-71.

42 Dominic M. Crossan, O.S.M., "Judges," in *The Jerome Biblical Commentary*, eds. Raymond E. Brown, S.S., et al. (Englewood Cliffs, New Jersey: Prentice-Hall, Inc., 1968), p. 152; and Soggin, *Judges*, p. 6.

43 Reed, *The Asherah*, p. 36.

44 Reed, *The Asherah*, p. 37.

45 Reed, *The Asherah*, p. 88.

46 De Moor, "Asherah," p. 441.

47 Reed, *The Asherah*, p. 54.

48 Ahlström, *Aspects of Syncretism*, pp. 11-12.

49 Raphael Patai, *The Hebrew Goddess* (New York: Avon, Discus Book, 1978), p. 48.

50 Eissfeldt, *The OT*, p. 265.

51 Soggin, *Judges*, p. 6.

52 William Foxwell Albright, *Yahweh and the Gods of Canaan: A Historical Analysis of Two Contrasting Faiths* (London: Athlone Press, 1968), p. 200.

53 Crossan, in *JBC*, p. 155.

54 Robert Boling, *Judges*, Anchor Bible, vol. 6A (New York: Doubleday & Co., 1975), p. 134.

55 Edward Lipinski, "The Goddess Atirat in Ancient Arabia, in Babylon, and in Ugarit," *Orientalia Lovaniensia Periodica* 3 (1972):112; Boling, *Judges*, p. 134 also describes Asherah as a sacred grove of trees, but without explanation.

56 Reed, *The Asherah*, as explained above under Ex 34:13 and Dt 16:21.

57 Peter Höffken, "Eine Bemerkung zum religionsgeschichtlichen Hintergrund von Dtn 6,4," *Biblische Zeitschrift* 28 (1984):88-93.

58 George E. Mendenhall, *The Tenth Generation: The Origins of the Biblical Tradition* (Baltimore: Johns Hopkins University Press, 1973), p. 218, nt. 6; and Ahlström, *Aspects of Syncretism*, p. 51.

59 Reed, *The Asherah*, p. 88.

Chapter 5

I Kings[1]

In his valuable study of the documentary hypothesis, M. Noth[2] declared that the books of Joshua, Judges, Samuel, and Kings were a literary unity introduced by the book of Deuteronomy. He based this assertion on their common theological themes which he saw as compiled from the accounts of various sources. Gray[3] added more detail to this theory. He pointed out that the central theme of all these books is the theme of covenant, the covenant to which the Israelites were sometimes faithful and at other times unfaithful. The theologians emphasized the national success which followed loyalty to the tradition of Moses, i.e., obedience to the covenant law, and the disaster which followed disloyalty to the law. Gray saw further unity among these books in the regular overlapping of their subject matter and in the schematic chronology which appears throughout them.

In the two books of Kings, these theologians, the deuteronomists, assessed fidelity by means of the criterion of cultic orthodoxy. This orthodoxy was the orthodoxy which stemmed from the principles of the reform of Josiah, c621. This reform was the focus of the deuteronomistic point of view[4].

In the books of Kings, the dominant themes of the deuteronomists emerge. They are, according to Gray:

> first, cultic orthodoxy according to principles familiar in the Book of Deuteronomy, centred in the Temple in Jerusalem, as the criterion of fidelity to the will of God for Israel, secondly, the fulfillment of the word of God in prophecy, and thirdly, divine retribution occasioned by infidelity to Deuteronomistic orthodoxy.[5]

Gray also notes (this is important for the discussion in this study) that these themes govern the material selected from the sources available to the deuteronomists. The deuteronomists determined the length of the treatment of their subjects according to the degree to which these subjects dealt with their themes. For example, anything which concerned the Temple and Jerusalem tends to be given a disproportionately longer treatment than other political matters which might to us be more important in the light of history. In addition, the deuteronomists especially expatiated matters which were derogatory to the Temple as the single and only seat of Yahweh in the nation.[6]

Thus, one would rightly expect that if there was a cult of Asherah among the Israelites, the deuteronomists would not only decry it, but would also focus on such an aberration in their theological histories, showing that dire consequences result from the worship of Asherah. The reader's expectation is not disappointed, because the deuteronomists deal with the Asherah problem straightforwardly in Kings. The evidence is found in the texts where deuteronomistic redactions are literarily most visible: in the introductions and conclusions to the descriptions of the reigns of various kings, and in the stereotypical language which assesses these same kings.

The theory of the composition of the books of Kings most popularly held by scholars today is that the compilation of sources took place in the pre-exilic era, perhaps not too long after Josiah, and that the redaction took place in exile. The pre-exilic compiler was concerned largely with the stories of the covenant people, and with how the separation of the kingdoms led to corruption in the southern kingdom. The exilic redactor was largely concerned with how, after the death of Josiah, the southern kingdom became corrupt.[7] Among other less frequently held views is that both the compilation and the redaction took place after the exile, $_{c}$500.[8] This study will assume the former opinion to be the more reliable.

Because the language used to describe the presence of Asherah in the cult is stereotypical, there arises the question of the historical veracity of these references. If the language is stereotypical and repetitive, does this suggest that it is perhaps part of some deuteronomistic tendency to exaggerate the facts, thus leading one to conclude that their references to Asherah were less historical and perhaps more a function of anger or disillusionment with the history of their people? Or should this language, on the contrary, suggest that the worship of Asherah was so deeply and continuously embedded in the religion of the people that the development of a stereotypical literary phraseology was inevitable?

Regarding the former, that the language suggests lack of historical veracity, one might construe the stereotypical and repetitive language as a kind of sloganizing, that is, the use of terms like 'asherah' as a slogan for idolatry, with little regard to whether the deity, Asherah, or her cult object of the same name were actually still in existence. While there is little doubt that Asherah was worshiped in the earlier centuries of the monarchy, it may be that, especially after the Josian reform, the deuteronomistic references to the later monarchy were more slogan than fact.

This theory is supported by the tendency of the deuteronomists to fictionalize certain other aspects of their religious history. For example, they attributed their theology to Moses. They also spoke of reviving the notion of holy war, even though it was a worn-out idea by the time of the deuteronomistic reform. It is possible that, by the later monarchy, the notion of Asherah was as worn-out as that of holy war. While both holy war and Asherah may have been firmly embedded in earlier history, by the time of the reforms they may have been outmoded and no longer used.

Regarding the latter supposition, that the stereotypical language suggests that Asherah was deeply embedded in Israelite religion for as long as the language was used, one might construe the Asherah language as the inevitable literary expression of pervasive Asherah worship. Rather than becoming fictionalized slogans, terms like 'asherah' remained what they always were, deuteronomistic reflections on what they saw as religions aberrations taking place in the cult, throughout the monarchy.

This theory is supported by some archaeological evidence. Asherah-like clay images have been dated from Israelite sites from the ninth to the early 6th centuries.[9] But more compelling is the literary argument. Included with Asherah in the 'slogan' formulas (cf. Chapter 3) are such terms as 'high place' and 'altar' and 'idol.' If this formula was a sloganized stereotype without true historical basis in the later monarchy, then one would expect to find little or no evidence of their existence in that period. But such is not the case. For example, regarding the high places, while archaeology can give good evidence that high places were in use during this later period, the texts themselves describe them with such language that, even though they appear to be stereotyped in some formulas, it suggests that they are actual places where cultic activities were taking place. II Kings 17:32 refers to the priests who staffed the high places in the late eighth century. In II Kings 23:8-9 the functions of the high places are described with interesting detail during the Josian reform, suggesting that even at that late date they had been in operation.

High places usually contained altars and other cult paraphernalia. Since the texts referred to these things in such a way that one supposes that they actually existed in the later monarchic period, and not as though they were merely fictionalized slogans, then one has to suppose also that the Asherah, a term used in formula along with these other terms which describe the cultic objects and places, is no more a fictionalized slogan than the other terms are. With this literary argument, one is led to believe that the Asherah, even though it appears in formulas with stereotypical language, was not, in the later monarchy, simply a deuteronomistic slogan used to refer to all the evils of idol worship, but rather was a representation of a continuing event in the monarchic history of Israel, that is, the worship of the goddess, Asherah.

Chapter 5 is concerned with the deuteronomistic history of I Kings. The texts will show that any suggestion that Asherah is a live tree or a grove of trees is untenable. They will reveal that both the people and some of their kings displayed a devoted allegiance to Asherah and her cult, that the cult was widespread, and that Asherah in the texts referred both to the goddess and her cult object, the wooden post. The term "high place" will be found here, a term which is both relevant and important as described reviously in this study. The texts will reveal that there was an active cult of Asherah in Bethel, and that this cult was supported by the Israelites, including the king. Finally, the texts will give evidence that there were prophets associated with the cult of Asherah, and that these prophets were supported by the king and were not punished for their cultic practices as were the prophets of Baal.

1. The Texts of I Kings

A. I Kings 14:15

> The Lord will strike Israel like a reed tossed about in the water and will pluck out Israel from this good land which he gave their fathers, scattering them beyond the River, because they made sacred poles [ʾăshērêhem] for themselves and thus provoked the Lord.

This text is a prophecy in the midst of the historical narrative. It is delivered to the king of Israel, Jeroboam. The prophet is Ahijah, who sent the prophetic message to the king through the king's wife.

It is generally agreed that this passage is the work of the deuteronomistic editor. Reed[10] noted a typically deuteronomistic comment; it is the king to whom are attributed the evils of the age. This is in contrast to the Chronicler who does not even mention the Asherahs in association with the king. Reed suspected that if it were not for the bias of the deuteronomistic editor, Asherah would not appear in this verse.

Gray viewed this text as part of the deuteronomistic elaboration on the earlier versions of the story, a segment which does not appear in the LXX. His reason:

> The language and the view of this catastrophe as divine chastisement for the sins of Jeroboam are characteristic of the deuteronomists, who, in the interests of Josiah's political and religious unification of the kingdom, were anxious to discredit the cult of Northern Israel.[11]

Responding directly to Reed's assertion that Asherah might not appear in this text if it were not for the bias of the deuteronomistic redactor, Ahlström[12] maintained that it is clear that Asherah was known since the earliest settlement, referring to Jg 3:7 et al. He argued that it is not only the deuteronomistic redactor who was aware of Asherah, but the history of the nation preceding him, at least as far back as the settlement, and possibly farther. It is, therefore, quite possible that the Asherah might have appeared in a version of the histories which preceded the deuteronomistic redactor.

Taking into account the text of 14:9 in which images of deities are condemned, Reed[13] said that the Asherah mentioned in this text is one of those images, a specific type of the idol images which incited God's anger. He also discussed the word ʿ*sh* which is frequently used to describe the act of making an Asherah (I Kg 14:15, 15:13, 16:33; II Kg 17:16, 21:3, 21:7; II Ch 15:16, 33:3; Is 17:8). Its usual meaning is "to construct" or "to make," as with Noah's ark (Gn 6), altars (II Kg 16:11), houses (II Sm 7:11), etc. Its use here implies that the Asherah did not grow of its own accord, as Lipinski[14] claimed, like a tree or grove of trees, but was constructed. It may have been wood, but it was not wood retaining its original form. It was shaped by human hands.

B. I Kings 14:23

> They, too, built for themselves high places, pillars, and sacred poles [ʾăshērîm][15], upon every high hill and under every green tree.

This text refers back to the king of Judah, Rehoboam. The "they" are the people of Judah under Rehoboam who bear the responsibility for their wrong-doing. This is again a deuteronomistic characteristic. Another such characteristic is in the following verse, 14:25, which implies that the wrong-doing of Judah was the reason for the invasion of Shishak of Egypt, which was about to occur.

Rehoboam was not alone in responsibility for the cult places. Ahlström[16] explained that Rehoboam was probably responding to the demands of the people, who seemed to have a fervent devotion to Asherah. The text also shows the deuteronomistic intolerance for cult places other than Jerusalem.

This text is a prime example of deuteronomistic editing. Gray[17] noted that it fits well into the pattern that the deuteronomist formed to present the stories: the name of the King of Judah, his age, the length of his reign, his mother's name, an appraisal of his reign according to deuteronomic principles, all of these using deuteronomic language. This verse is part of the appraisal.

Reed[18] made several comments which serve to explain this verse. First he noted that *bnh*, which is translated "to build" or "to construct," suggests that the Asherah, like the high places and the pillars, was an object constructed by humans, not a living tree or a grove. Second, he said that the location of the Asherah "under every green tree" also suggests that it was itself not a tree, much less a grove of trees. Reed might have added that to decry the placement of Asherahs under every green tree and upon every high hill might have been a slight exaggeration; nevertheless it points to the impression of the author that the worship of Asherah was spread all throughout the land of Judah.

The meaning of "high place" has been important in this study. Reed[19] suggested that it is nearly synonymous with the sanctuary. He noted that there are 12 occurrences of Asherah and high place together in the Hebrew Bible.[20] This shows that Asherah and high place are both cultic accessories, but that they are not one and the same. They are spatially related to one another. The Asherah usually is "on" or "in" the high place. Moreover, both are condemned by the text.

The Asherah is here the apparatus of the fertility cult associated with the mother-goddess Asherah. Gray[21] suggested that perhaps the connection between the pole and Asherah is that the stylized tree symbolizes the productivity and receptivity which, as found in nature, is stimulated by rain. Rain was the province of her consort, Baal. Gray also brought to mind theophoric names like Abdaserat, found regularly in the Amarna Tablets, showing how Asherah was an integral part of life.

C. I Kings 15:13

> He also deposed his grandmother Maacah from her position as queen mother, because she had made an outrageous object for Asherah. Asa cut

down this object and burned it in the Kidron Valley. 14The high places did not disappear; yet Asa's heart was entirely with the Lord as long as he lived.

Maacah was a wife of Rehoboam, the wife who bore Rehoboam's successor, Abijam, who was succeeded by Asa. Her descent can be traced from the Aramaean district, which is inland and northeast from Tyre, definitely a non-Israelite territory. Ahlström[22] suggested that there is a parallel between Maacah of the southern kingdom and Jezebel in the northern kingdom regarding the introduction of foreign cult into Israel. In line with this parallel, Ellis[23] noted that the title of queen mother can be rendered as "powerful lady."

Regarding the identity of Asherah in the text, Gray[24] is quite firm in calling her the mother-goddess of the Canaanite fertility cult. Reed[25] also said that Asherah here refers to the deity herself, the goddess whose image was destroyed. Although less specific, Ben-Sasson[26] linked the image with the Tyrean goddess, Asherah, whom he said was well-known at the time.

Regarding the image of Asherah, Patai[27] suggested that the image mentioned in the text was probably in the Temple itself, although the text does not say so. Another suggestion of Patai's, equally interesting, is the result of a question.[28] He asked why the Asherahs are first mentioned as being destroyed and not set up. His answer was that perhaps this is because their existence was known as far back as the pre-monarchic period, before the beginning date of this deuteronomistic history.

The verb *ʿsh* is used in this text with the accusative and the preposition *l*. Ahlström[29] discussed this point and argued that it means "to do something for someone." With this in mind, it becomes evident that the cult object of this text was set up "for" Asherah. He concluded from this that the *mipᵉleṣet* is that object. This is only one among many indications of the syncretistic character of the Yahweh cult.

Lipinski[30] described the *mipᵉleṣet* of this text as a phallic emblem, referring to the Hebrew root *blṭ*, meaning "to protrude." This is a doubtful interpretation. There is no need to extend its meaning this far. The same expression could apply just as well to a wooden post representing Asherah without necessarily being a phallic symbol. Moreover, since Asherah is female, why would she be represented by a phallic symbol?

A final note on this text: The LXX parallel to this verse in II Ch 15:16 names Astarte in place of Asherah. This might have been the product of the LXX's translator(s), but it might also have been in the Hebrew *Vorlage* from which the translation was made. This is one of many signs of the later confusion between these two deities.

D. I Kings 16:33

> Ahab erected an altar to Baal in the temple of Baal which he built in Samaria, 33and also made a sacred pole [ʾăshērāh]...

This verse is attributable to the deuteronomistic compiler/editor. Eissfeldt and Gray[31] argued that the primary reason for this is that it carries a deuteronomistic theme. The suggestion is made in 31-33 that the marriage to Jezebel is a precursor to the clash with Elijah, and the oracle of doom which Elijah uttered against Ahab's house. The deuteronomistic editor is known to have regularly assigned the king responsibility for the cultic aberrations of the people.

Ahab acted at the recommendation of Jezebel, but for political reasons. Commenting on this, Patai[32] recalled that the father of Jezebel was Ethbaal, King of Sidon. Sidon had been a known center of Asherah worship for at least five centuries before Ahab. For Ahab to erect an Asherah in his own territory would have served to consolidate the alliance with Ethbaal which had first been struck by Ahab's marriage with Jezebel. Gray[33] noted that there is a parallel between Ahab's building houses of worship for his Canaanite wife and Solomon's building houses of worship for his foreign wives, which was also done for political reasons (I Kg 11:7).

The worship at this temple in Samaria calls to mind an interesting observation. Patai[34] argued that it was known to be such a center from as far back as Abraham, who himself worshiped near there (Gn 12:8).

In identifying the Asherah in this text, Ellis[35] stated that the Asherah was a symbol of the female divinity in the Baal religion. He equated this with the stone pillar, which was the symbol of the male divinity. It can thus be concluded from his statements that the Asherah, who is a goddess, and her cultic symbol, which is the post, had one and the same name: Asherah.

Following Ahab's construction of the Asherah, there is no mention of its removal for many years. Patai[36] noted, however, that during the reign of Joram, son of Ahab, there was a reform in which the pillar was removed (II Kg 3:2). Patai observed that while the pillar was removed, the Asherah was not even mentioned. He suggested that Joram did not remove the Asherah. If this were true, as Patai said, this is another example of the Asherah being considered an appropriate adoption from the Canaanite religion, while Baal worship was considered an aberration.

E. I Kings 18:19

> Now summon all Israel to me on Mount Carmel as well as the 450 prophets of Baal and the 400 prophets of Asherah who eat at Jezebel's table.

This is part of the famous story of Elijah and the prophets, their duel of deities on Mount Carmel. While the name Asherah appears only in this verse, the whole story is of value to this study. It occupies all of chapter 18.

Some have considered the mention of Asherah an addition. Würthwein[37] argued that it was the result of scholarly surmise on the part of the redactor. It is said that if it had been a part of the original story, it would also have been mentioned in verse 22, which is its parallel. Another commentator who considered this an addition is Kapelrud.[38] He said that it was added by the redactor to show the familiar association of Baal and Asherah, but has no relevance to the text. Olyan added to this argument the observation that the editor appears to be expanding the text in a natural fashion after being schooled in deuteronomistic anti-Asherah ideology.[39]

In the LXX, the prophets are included not only in verse 19 but also in verse 22, as *oi prophētai toû 'ălsous*. Thus the LXX viewed the prophets of Asherah not only as present on the Mount during the contest (19), but as participants in the contest (22). Reed[40] claimed that, given a choice between accepting the mention of Asherah in verse 22 of the LXX as an addition, and its mention in verse 19 as an omission from the Hebrew text, he would favor the latter. His choice is based on Jg 3:7 which states that Israel was engaged in the service of both the Baals and the Asherahs, and on the Ugaritic literature in which Asherah was a consort goddess. He maintained that she should be considered a consort whether being served by Canaanites or Israelites, because that is her cultic role.

The term *nabiim* in verse 19 is applied equally to the cultic servants of Baal and the cultic servants of Asherah. Gray[41] said that this implies that these prophets had common features. Among the features usually associated with the *nabiim* were such things as ecstasy, oracles, and speaking to the deities on behalf of the people. Such can be presumed for these prophets as well.

That there were in fact cultic personnel associated with Asherah in Canaan has been satisfactorily shown by McCurley and Albright[42]. Albright referred to a 15th century text from Taanach which shows that there was a prophetic function attached to the Asherah cult, that of giving oracles. McCurley showed that the rituals of the prophets of Baal in chapter 18 are part of a Baalistic ritual, paralleling the Baal myth. The rituals had for their purpose to end the drought of three years (17:1, 18:1), a problem which was the responsibility of the rain god, Baal. In time of drought, it was understood that Baal was dead and needed to be brought back to life through ritual. To the extent that McCurley is correct, this would support the theory that the mention of Asherah prophets is not an addition to verse 19. If the Asherah prophets were present at the scene, as stated in verse 19, they would likely not have been mentioned in verse 22 which portrayed the ceremony of reviving Baal. They would have had no part to play in that ceremony. Thus the failure to mention them in verse 22 does not suggest that they were not there.

The text says that the prophets ate at the table of Jezebel. Ellis and Gray[43] both commented on this fact. Ellis said that eating at her table indicated that they were subsidized by Jezebel, implying that they were official in status. Gray saw another angle. He suggested that, since they ate at Jezebel's table while at the Carmel location, one might say that the Carmel territory was given to her husband, Ahab, as a marriage dowry, and would therefore be part of his territory and in close association with his activities. Thus the official prophets enjoyed the hospitality of their host, king Ahab, at this distant location.

And what of the fate of the prophets of Asherah? Patai[44] observed that although the Baal prophets were slaughtered, the fate of the Asherah prophets went unmentioned. He suggested that they were not part of the contest, that no harm befell them, and that they must have been free to continue in their cult. Freedman agrees with this argument when he asks, "What happened to Asherah and her prophets? Nothing."[45] Elijah considered the Baal prophets and their ritual to be a danger to the cult and had them punished, yet demanded no punishment for the Asherah prophets. Evidently Elijah did not see them as a danger to the cult of Yahweh, and perhaps saw them as representatives of a goddess who was a tolerable female counterpart to Yahweh in cultic service.

In the succeeding reigns of Ahaziah, Joram, Jehu, and Joahaz, no mention is made of the destruction of the Asherah image in Samaria or of the prophets of Asherah being stopped. Patai[46] noted that Joram had removed the pillar (II Kg 3:2), but the Asherah was reported as still standing during the reign of Joahaz (II Kg 13:6). The implication, he maintained, is that all of these were continued and accepted. Apparently the Israelites were not being accused of abandoning Yahweh for foreign gods, but of dividing their allegiance between Yahweh and the other deities, Baal and Asherah (18:31). They saw no problem in combining these allegiances.

About the names of Ahab's sons, Ahaziah, Joram, etc., Bright[47] made an interesting observation. He showed that they are Yahwist names, indicating that Ahab was an adherent of Yahwism. But the official status of the Baal and the Asherah prophets, he noted, demonstrate that his Yahwism was not pure in any sense, but was a syncretism of broad proportion. Gray[48] agreed, saying that the people of Israel saw no apparent conflict or incompatibility in worshiping Yahweh, Asherah, and Baal at the same time.

In verse 39, after Yahweh had won the contest, the victory cry was shouted, "Yahweh is God." Even though the worship of Asherah apparently continued unhindered, Asherah was not mentioned as a victor or even a living deity. There was no reason to mention her here. The contest did not involve Asherah, but only Yahweh and Baal. Since Yahweh won, Yahweh was proclaimed the victor. Perhaps the people saw no conflict in proclaiming Yahweh their God and continuing to honor Asherah as their goddess.

From this first of the two deuteronomistic books of Kings we have gathered more information about Asherah. In spite of any attempts at reform, Asherah was served continuously from at least as early as the settlement till the time when this First Book of Kings ends, c850 B.C.E.

Asherah was considered both a deity and a cult object. This object was the wooden post made by human hands, not a grove of trees.

The people of Judah and Israel had a devotion to Asherah which they did not view as being in conflict with their worship of Yahweh, but rather in harmony with it. They thought of Asherah as the divine consort of Yahweh.

Asherah worship was widespread in Judah and Israel. There is evidence that certain rituals accompanied Asherah service and that there were active prophets of Asherah in the region. This deity, who had been known for centuries in Tyre and Sidon, was now being worshiped in the temples of Bethel and even Jerusalem.

Notes

1 The texts from I and II Kings should properly appear together because of the literary unity of the two books. It is only to avoid creating a cumbersome unit that they are divided into two separate chapters.

2 Martin Noth, *Überlieferungsgeschichtliche Studien I* (Tübingen: M. Niemeyer, 1957), section 12.

3 John Gray, *I & II Kings: A Commentary*, 2nd ed. (Philadelphia: Westminster Press, 1970), pp. 2-4.

4 Gray, *I & II Kings*, pp. 5 and 37; and J. Robinson, *The First Book of Kings*, Cambridge Bible Commentary, vol. 25 (Cambridge: Cambridge University Press, 1972), pp. 9 and 12.

5 Gray, *I & II Kings*, p. 9.

6 Gray, *I & II Kings*, pp. 9, 13-14. See also Robinson, *The First Book of Kings*, p. 8; and Simon J. DeVries, *1 Kings*, World Biblical Commentary, vol. 12 (Waco, Texas: World Books, 1985), pp. xxix-xxxviii.

7 A. Jepsen, *Die Quellen des Königsbuches*, 2nd ed. (Halle: M. Niemeyer, 1956), pp. 76ff.; Robinson, *The First Book of Kings*, pp. 13-14; and Gray, *I & II Kings*, p. 9.

8 G. Hölscher, "Das Buch der Könige, seine Quellen und seine Redaktion," *Forschungen zur religion und Literatur des Alten und Neuen Testaments*, vol 36 (Göttingen: Vandenhoeck & Ruprecht, 1927; and Noth, *Überlieferungs-geschichtliche Studien*.

9 See below, Chapter 9. See also Chapter 10, which suggests that certain inscriptions about Asherah are dated from the later part of the monarchy.

10 William L. Reed, *The Asherah in the Old Testament* (Fort Worth: Texas Christian University, 1949), p. 60.

11 Gray, *I & II Kings*, p. 339. Peter F. Ellis, C.SS.R., "1-2 Kings," in *Jerome Biblical Commentary*, eds. Raymond E. Brown, et al. (Englewood Cliffs, New Jersey: Prentice Hall, Inc., 1968), p. 192 agrees that this is a deuteronomistic redaction.

12 G. W. Ahlström, *Aspects of Syncretism in Israelite Religion* (Lund: C. W. K. Gleerup, 1963), p. 51.

13 Reed, *The Asherah*, pp. 30, 93.

14 See above under Jg 6:25-30.

15 Note that 'asherim' is grammatically parallel to 'Elohim.'

16 Ahlström, *Aspects of Syncretism*, p. 10.

17 Gray, *I & II Kings*, pp. 340, 342-3.

18 Reed, *The Asherah*, p. 30.

19 Reed, *The Asherah*, pp. 46-8. For a full treatment of bama, see Patrick H. Vaughan, *The meaning of "BAMA" in the Old Testament* (Cambridge, England: Cambridge University Press, 1974). For a further discussion of the nature of the high place, see W. Boyd Barrick, "What Do We Really Know about 'High Places'?" *Svensk Exegetisk Arsbok* 45 (1980): 50-57.

20 Actually there are 15. They are I Kg 14:23, 15:13; II Kg 17:10, 18:4, 21:3, 23:4, 23:15; II Ch 14:3, 15:16, 17:6, 31:1, 33:3, 33:19, 34:3, Jr 17:2.

21 Gray, *I & II Kings*, pp. 342-3.

22 Ahlström, *Aspects of Syncretism*, p. 59.

23 Ellis, "1-2 Kings," p. 193. For further discussion on the role of the queen mother, see Niels-Erick A. Andreasen, "The Role of Queen Mother in Israelite Society," *Catholic Biblical Quarterly* 45 (1983): 179-194.

24 Gray, *I & II Kings*, p. 350.

25 Reed, *The Asherah*, p. 61.

26 H. H. Ben-Sasson, ed., *A History of the Jewish People* (Cambridge, Mass.: Harvard University Press, 1976), p. 118.

27 Raphael Patai, "The Goddess Asherah," *Journal of Near Eastern Study* 24 (1965): 48. Reed, *The Asherah*, p. 61 also mentions this.

28 Raphael Patai, *The Hebrew Goddess* (New York: Avon, Discus Book, 1978), p. 34.

29 Ahlström, *Aspects of Syncretism*, p. 58.

30 Edward Lipinski, "The Goddess of Atirat in Ancient Arabia, in Babylon, and in Ugarit," *Orientalia Lovaniensia Periodica* 3 (1972): 113.

31 Otto Eissfeldt, *The Old Testament: An Introduction*, trans. P. R. Ackroyd (New York: Harper & Row, 1965), p. 291; and Gray, *I & II Kings*, p. 362.

32 Patai, *The Hebrew Goddess*, p. 27.

33 Gray, *I & II Kings*, p. 369.

34 Patai, *The Hebrew Goddess*, p. 31.

35 Ellis, "1-2 Kings," p. 194.

36 Patai, "The Goddess Asherah," p. 46.

37 Ernst Würthwein, *The Text of the Old Testament: An Introduction to the Biblia Hebraica*, trans. Errol F. Rhodes (Grand Rapids: William B. Eerdmans, 1979), p. 110.

38 Arvid S. Kapelrud, *The Ras Shamra Discoveries and the Old Testament*, trans. G. W. Anderson (Tulsa, Oklahoma: University of Oklahoma Press, 1963).

39 Saul M. Olyan. *Asherah and the Cult of Yahweh in Israel*, SBL Monograph Series, No. 34, (Atlanta, Georgia: Scholars Press, 1988), p. 8.

40 Reed, *The Asherah*, p. 55.

41 Gray, *I & II Kings*, p. 393.

42 William Foxwell Albright, "A Prince of Taanach in the Fifteenth Century B.C.," *Bulletin of the American Schools of Oriental Research* 94 (1944): 12-27; Foster R. McCurley, *Ancient Myths and Biblical Faith: Scriptural Transformations* (Philadelphia: Fortress Press, 1983), p.80. Roland De Vaux, *The Bible and the Ancient Near East*, trans. Damian McHugh (New York: Doubleday, 1971), pp.238-51 gives more detailed information about this ritual in

agreement with McCurley. See also Leah Bronner, *The Stories of Elijah and Elisha as Polemics Against Baal Worship* (Leiden: E. J. Brill, 1968).

43 Ellis, "1-2 Kings," p. 194; Gray, *I & II Kings*, p. 385.

44 Patai, *The Hebrew Goddess*, pp. 27-28.

45 David Noel Freedman, "Yahweh of Samaria and His Asherah," *Biblical Archaeologist*, (December, 1989): 241-249.

46 Patai, *The Hebrew Goddess*, pp. 29-31.

47 John Bright, *A History of Israel*, 3rd ed. (Philadelphia: Westminster, 1981), p. 246.

48 Gray, *I & II Kings*, p. 385.

Chapter 6

II Kings

Chapter 6 completes the examination of Asherah texts and the search for information about her cult in the deuteronomistic books of I and II Kings. The texts of II Kings show that Asherah worship was more acceptable to the Israelites than Baal worship and that the official purges of foreign influence from Yahwism were more effective in eliminating Baal worship than Asherah worship. In spite of harsh attempts to eliminate the Asherah cult, Asherah worship could not be eradicated and remained a widespread, popular religious practice among the people of Israel and Judah. She was even worshiped in the Temple of Jerusalem where her idol, the wooden post, stood near the altar and where her cultic services were performed. This association of Asherah and Yahweh suggests again that they were considered a divine couple, heavenly consorts. A new interpretation of II Kg 23:7 will show that there was a sexual ritual associated with the Asherah cult in which women who were childless approached male sexual ritualizers at the Jerusalem Temple. In these rituals the males would impregnate the women in the name of Asherah, the mother-goddess.

1. The Texts of II Kings

A. II Kings 13:6

Nevertheless they did not desist from the sins which the house of Jeroboam had caused Israel to commit, but persisted in them. The sacred pole [hā'ăshērāh] also remained standing in Samaria.

This passage is deuteronomistic. Gray[1] showed this when he observed that the general pattern of the deuteronomistic accounts of the kings is operative in this chapter and when he saw a reflection of the tone of the deuteronomist as it is found in Jg 13:4-6. Israel had been granted a reprieve, but it was only a temporary postponement of their punishment. As they are accused in this verse, they had not put aside all of their foreign worship, but only some of it.

The verb ʿ*md*, "to stand," is used with Asherah. Reed and Patai[2] both made comments about its implications. Reed demonstrated that its meaning suggests more than its mere placement, as for example a house stands, but that it implies a standing erect. The fact that the Asherah stood erect reinforces the notion that it was a post, and further defies any attempts to describe it as a grove of trees. Patai noted that this Asherah, first erected by Ahab, whose reign began $_c$874 (I Kg 16:33), stood continuously in Samaria through the reign of Jehoahaz, who died $_c$797. The Asherah stood, then, through the time of the opposition of Elijah to Baalistic worship. It would appear, then, that Asherah worship was more acceptable in Yahwism than Baal worship.

Jehu (II Kg 9-10) had engaged in a heavy-handed purging of the Baal cult from the nation. In 10:18-27 he destroyed the Baal sanctuary and its paraphernalia. His act was in reaction to Ahab's sins and their source, Jezebel. However, he did not destroy the Asherah, as 13:6 shows. Ahlström[3] concluded from this that the Asherah was not seen as associated only with Jezebel, i.e., it was not viewed as something which was introduced by this foreign queen. If it had been viewed as part of the foreign Baal cult, surely it would have been purged along with all the rest. No, Asherah was not seen as a foreign deity, like Baal, but as a familiar one, like Yahweh.

Regarding personal names in this period, it seems that the Israelite names recorded from this time were formed half with Baal derivations and half with Yahwist. Albright[4] claimed that this is a sign of the widespread allegiance to Baal which some were attempting to purge. It is noteworthy that the purgation was more hearty for Baal than for Asherah.

B. II Kings 17:10

> 9...They built high places in all their settlements, the watchtowers as well as the walled cities. 10They set up pillars and sacred poles [wa'ăshērîm] for themselves on every high hill and under every leafy tree.

This verse is a deuteronomistic segment, chapter 17, which according to Eissfeldt[5] has a pre-deuteronomic basis, of which verses 7-20 are a deuteronomistic expansion. Gray[6] agreed that this is a deuteronomistic segment, especially because it describes the calamitous fate of Israel, being conquered by Assyria, as a result of involvement with the foreign cults.

This verse points to Dt 12:2, "Destroy without fail every place on the high mountains, on the hills, and under every leafy tree where the nations you are to disposses worship their gods." Ellis[7] noted that this verse precedes an important deuteronomistic command to wipe out Asherah along with all foreign practices in the land of Judah. The influence of the deuteronomist is strong. Ellis also saw this verse pointing to Jr 3:6, "The Lord said to me in the days of King Josiah: Have you seen what she did, that faithless Israel, how she went up on every high hill, and under every green tree and there played the harlot?"(RSV)

Yaṣṣibû, a Hiphil form of *nṣb*, is a word commonly used to describe the 'setting up' of columns and the erecting of altars (Gn 33:20, II Sam 18:17). Reed[8] showed how it applies here. It again stresses that Asherah was no grove or tree, but a cult object set in an upright position by human beings.

The description of the location of the Asherahs is expansive, "on every high hill and under every leafy tree." It leads one to see that the deuteronomist was thoroughly disgusted at the extent of Asherah worship at the time of Hoshea, who was the king of Israel under whom the abuses named in this verse took place. And that the deuteronomist, who was doubtlessly embarrassed by this fact, would admit to such widespread abuse lends further credence to the fact that the abuse was actually taking place.

C. II Kings 17:16

> They disregarded all the commandments of the Lord, their God, and made for themselves two molten calves; they also made a sacred pole [ʾăshērāh] and worshiped all the host of heaven, and served Baal.

Asherah is used in the singular in this verse. This is in close proximity to 17:10, in which it was used in the plural to describe its widespread distribution. In this verse, Patai[9] pointed out, it demonstrates the central and elevated role that Asherah played in Israelite worship. Verses 10 and 16, when considered together, express the breadth and the depth of Asherah worship in the territory of Israel.

Calves represent Baal in the ancient Ugaritic cult. Reed[10] noted that the making of the molten image, *massēkāh*, of two calves suggests that the people were worshiping idols, in this case representing Baal. Gray[11] suggested that because *massēkāh* is singular and describes what must have been two images of calves, each placed in different locations (Dan and Bethel, as in I Kg 12:29), therefore this use of the term can be considered an addition. Gray does admit that there is a slight possibility that the singular is a collective noun, but it is slight.

At the same time Gray discussed the host of heaven. He said that it is a reference to the astral cult of Mesopotamia. II Kg 16:10 implies that the introduction of the astral cult into Palestine was a sign of vassalage to Assyria who had subjugated them. Part of the settlement required assumption of the religion of the victors, so the king established worship of their whole host of heaven. This added more fuel to the fires of the Yahwists who subscribed to Deuteronomic principles. They saw every addition to the service of foreign deities as a further deterioration of their true religion.

D. II Kings 18:4

> It was he who removed the high places, shattered the pillars, and cut down the sacred poles [hāʾăshērāh].[12] He smashed the bronze serpent called Ne-

hushtan which Moses had made, because up to that time the Israelites were burning incense to it.

Judah seemed ripe for reform. The nation which had subjugated her was in a weakened state. Sargon II of Assyria was beset with rebellion in many subject states, so many that he could not repress them all. He was not able to withstand the brazen rebellion that Hezekiah encouraged in Judah.

The cultic reforms of Hezekiah were in tune with his general policy which combined nationalism and Yahwistic zeal. Bright[13] noted that these policies were signs of open rebellion against the Assyrians. He suggested that these reforms were at first slight, to test Assyrian reaction, and sweeping only when the independence movement gained momentum.

Hezekiah made a heroic effort to eliminate Asherah worship and other foreign influences from the land. Aharoni[14] noted that Hezekiah was the first king to limit the functions of local cult places by centralizing the offering of sacrifices in Jerusalem 18:22, 24). Rosenbaum[15] noted that the deuteronomist mentions the reforms of Hezekiah in only three places, in 18:4, 16, and 22, in spite of their importance. Of these three, two are rather vague. It is only in 18:4 that there is mention of the specific reforms enacted by Hezekiah in Judah. This verse, observed Reed,[16] is a summary statement. It is characteristic of the work one might expect of a later scribe, such as the deuteronomist. Kjeseth[17] explained the work of the deuteronomist a little further. The redactor used this verse as the historical kernel assembled into his work, preceded by the typical deuteronomistic introduction of 18:1-3. This was the only tradition that the redactor had at hand regarding the specific religious reforms of Hezekiah. This stereotypical language, as noted in the introduction to Chapter 5, does not suggest that the Asherah is present only as a fictionalized slogan, but rather, indicates how deeply Asherah worship was imbedded in the cult.

The text has an enduring awareness of the worship of serpents, extending from Nm 21:6. Kjeseth, continuing his discussion, noted that the etymology of Nehushtan, the name given to the serpent in this verse, is a combination of serpent (*n*ᵉ*ḥaš*) and copper (*nᵉḥošet*), as in Nm 21:9. Ringgren[18] saw Nehushtan as a cultic aberration, the appropriate object of Hezekiah's reform, which was to be destroyed along with the pillars and the Asherahs which were the apotheosis of wood and stone.

In the structure of this verse there is a parallel between Asherah and Nehushtan, and presumably the pillars. Patai[19] suggested that they were all standing in the Temple as cultic worship objects.

There is a question about the origin and meaning of the use of the serpent in the Hebrew cult. After examining archaeological evidence, Joines concluded that "the practice of repelling serpents by a serpent image was common to [the Egyptians],"[20] but that this same use was not found either in Palestine or Mesopotamia. On the other hand, use of bronze serpents in Palestine or Mesopotamia was a part of the fertility cults, a use which was not found in Egypt. She concluded from this that the Nehushtan of II Kg 18:4

> is unrelated to Moses' bronze serpent except by popular tradition. There is reason to believe that Moses carried a bronze serpent, but as a means of sympathetic magic to repel serpents, a motif he received from the Egyptians. Nehushtan was a fertility symbol of Canaanite and Mesopotamian background adopted by the Israelite cult to depict the fecundizing power of Yahweh.[21]

De Vaux[22] agreed that Nehushtan was borrowed from the Canaanites, and that their use of it was falsely claimed to have originated with Moses. From this he made the interesting suggestion that perhaps the story in Nm 21 was an invention created to explain the text of II Kg 18:4, which attributes the use of the serpent to Moses.

Another scholar, Saul Olyan, suggests another association between Asherah and Nehushtan. Since as the Lady of Elat, Asherah was depicted with a serpant, and since the Ugaritic form of her name sometimes includes the phrase *hwt*, and since the Hebrew for Eve is *hawwa*, it is entirely possible that the image of Eve and the serpent are in some fashion a parallel with Asherah and the serpent.[23]

E. II Kings 21:3

He rebuilt the high places which his father Hezekiah had destroyed. He erected altars to Baal and also set up a sacred pole [ʾăshērāh][24], as Ahab, King of Israel, had done. He worshiped and served the whole host of heaven.

That this passage is the product of the deuteronomistic compiler is generally agreed upon.[25]

The altars and high places are mostly synonynous, at least in the eyes of the redactor. Vaughan[26] noted that in 21:4 the altars are described as being erected in the temple proper, whereas the high places are scattered throughout the countryside. The mention of both the high places and the altars in 21:3 does not contradict his assertion that they are synonymous. The expression seems parallel in both instances.

There are two theories as to why Manasseh reverted to the foreign ways after his father Hezekiah's reform. Bright[27] suggested that he made this total break from his father in order to pay homage to the deities of those who were still officially his overlords, the Assyrians. This is a limping theory, because Assyria was too weak to enforce its grip on Judah. The only support for this theory is the reference to the heavenly hosts, the astral deities of Assyria. This, however, can be explained as an attractive vestigial practice, not necessarily related to any political intent of Manasseh.

The second theory is stronger. It relies not on Judah's connection with Assyria, which was all but severed, but with her connection with the Canaanites, their neighbors. Ringgren[28] saw this as a deliberate attempt on the part of Manasseh to unite the Yahwists with the Canaanite cult.

The Asherah was the only idol introduced into the Temple by Manasseh. Patai[29] argued that the serpent had lost significance and did not need to be replaced. But Asherah was still dear to the hearts of the people. Patai was tempted to conjecture the mythical reason: to provide a consort for Yahweh, since Yahweh was seen to be a local (Jerusalem) manifestation of Baal.

The text of 21:3 refers to Ahab of Israel. The reference is found in I Kg 16:32ff. The comparison of Manasseh to the Samaritan heretic is an obvious detraction of Manasseh, not at all surprising from the deuteronomist.

Thus Manasseh is portrayed in this text as a supporter of Asherah worship, and hence an enemy of deuteronomistic Yahwism. This text is better understood when considered with the next, II Kg 21:7.

F. II Kings 21:7

> The Asherah idol [pesel hā'ăshērāh] he had made he set up in the Temple, of which the Lord had said to David and to his son Solomon: "In this Temple and in Jerusalem, which I have chosen out of all the tribes of Israel, I shall place my name forever."

The term Asherah is repeated here, as from verse three. In these two verses, describing the horrible things that Manasseh constructed, only Asherah is repeated, giving it a mark of importance. Reed[30] noted that in 21:3 it was called simply an Asherah, whereas in this verse it is called an Asherah idol. De Moor[31] made the same observation, but added that there is also no sharp differentiation betweem them, such that the deity and her cult object were not distinguished one from another. Ringgren[32] agreed that while the terms are not distinguished, one must note that the deity and the cult object are not one and the same, that the deity was seen to be the point of departure for the name of the cult object. Yamashita[33] said that the genitive construction of Asherah is a little ambiguous in this verse, but admitted that it suggests that the Asherah is here more than an image.

There is no parallel in the Hebrew Bible to *pesel hāʾ*ᵃ*šērāh*, in the sense of a *pesel* of some other deity. Reed claimed that this is a direct reference to an image of the goddess Asherah. He noted that it could be called both an image of Asherah (21:7) or simply an Asherah (21:3). Hence the author (or redactor) "may not have distinguised in verse 7 between the image and the *numen.*"[34] Gray said that "from the use of *pesel* ('a graven image') it is obvious that Asherah was a goddess and not an inanimate object."[35] His comment brings back to mind Lipinski's attempt to defend his thesis that the Asherah was a sanctuary.[36] In order to defend his thesis, he is forced to say that Asherah in 21:7 refers to an idol or emblem placed in the sanctuary. This argument is unsuccessful because he does not explain how the Asherah, a sanctuary for him, could have been built in the already existing Temple sanctuary. He also failed to give the identity of the deity for whom this idol or emblem was built. Furthermore, he does not explain why the idol is named after a sanctuary and not a deity, since according to his theory the Asherah is a sanctuary.

An understanding of this verse is helpful in interpreting the meaning of *laʾăšērāh* found in I Kg 15:13. Since this verse teaches that there was such a thing as an Asherah idol, one might suspect that the idol of I Kg 15:13 was just the same, made "for Asherah." Reed[37] agreed, saying that it was an idol dedicated to the goddess Asherah.

Placing the Asherah in the Temple implies associating her with Yahweh. Reed[38] said that worship of Asherah and Yahweh were probably simultaneous but not connected. This is an unwarranted hesitation for Reed. There is no reason, in the light of the biblical evidence, to refrain from suggesting that Asherah and Yahweh were worshiped together, even as a couple. Dohmen[39] agreed with this suggestion. He maintained that the Asherah in this verse implies a female deity which was placed, through her cult object, in the Temple with her natural consort, Yahweh.

Thus the Asherah is not only an idol, but a goddess worshiped by the people in the Jerusalem Temple. They considered her to be the consort of Yahweh.

G. II Kings 23:4

Then the king commanded the high priest Hilkiah, his vicar, and the doorkeepers to remove from the Temple of the Lord all the objects that had been made for Baal, Asherah [wᵉlā'ăshērāh], and the whole host of heaven. He had these burned outside Jerusalem on the slopes of the Kidron and their ashes carried to Bethel.

The king in this text is Josiah, the great reformer. Aharoni[40] observed that this verse indicates that Bethel is in the hands of Josiah. It had long been under control of the Northern Kingdom. But now that the territory to the north of Judah was the Assyrian province of Samaria, Josiah was challenging the rule of Assyria as Hezekiah had done. Josiah had won control of the province of Samaria at least as far north as Bethel.

Eissfeldt has assigned this text and all the following Asherah texts of II Kings to the materials found in the history of the kings of Judah. These materials were assembled by the deuteronomistic compiler. Gray[41] agreed with this contention in full.

Who were Hilkiah, the vicar, and the doorkeepers? They were all cult officials. Ringgren[42] noted that the vicar was the second priest, the assistant to the chief priest, Hilkiah. Goulder[43] suggested that the doorkeepers were the Korahites. De Vaux[44] described all of these, the chief priest, his assistant, and the three doorkeepers as the highest priestly officials of the Temple.

The host of heaven appear again in this text. There is some debate as to whom they represent. Bright and Ellis[45] followed the interpretataion that applies to earlier verses such as 17:16, describing the host of heaven as the astral deities of Assyria. Ahlström[46] has introduced a new interpretation that should be noticed. He contended that the host of heaven refers to ancient Canaanite symbols which had been present at the Temple since its construction. He said that this explanation is equally as plausible as the Assyrian deity explanation. One can support Ahlström's theory by noting that Hiram, who built the Temple for Solomon, came from Tyre, a known center of Canaanite worship. Asherah was the goddess of Tyre. Nevertheless, the debate between the Mesopotamian and the Canaanite explanations of the hosts of heaven remains unsettled. Ahlström also noted that 23:4 also implies that the Baal cycle, the ritual of the renewal of life, was actually being enacted inside the Temple of Jerusalem.

Among the items destroyed by Josiah were cult objects, *hakkelîm*, which can be described as utensils or vessels of the kind used in cultic rituals. Reed[47] noted that these had been made for

Baal, Asherah, and the host of heaven. This is a rare insight into the nature of Asherah worship. If cultic vessels or utensils were used in her service, then there were rituals that accompanied their use. Asherah worship was, therefore, part of the formal worship ceremonies that took place in the Temple of Jerusalem.

The word for "slopes" is *šadᵉmōt* is translated "slopes," the slopes of the Kidron valley. Lehmann[48] made an interesting suggestion regarding the origin of this term. He said that it developed from two other terms, *śᵉdē mōt*, which mean "fields of Mot." Lehmann's suggestion seems to be an appropriate description of the location of Kidron, since Kidron was earlier used as the place of immolation for Mot, the Canaanite god of drought and sterility, and later as the place for burning the refuse of the Temple.

While Asherah is mentioned here with Baal, such is not the case in a number of other verses. Pritchard and Kuenen[49] both made this observation. Pritchard noted that it is usually Ashtaroth (Astarte) who is mentioned with Baal (Jg 2:13, 10:6; I Sam 7:4, 12:10; etc.). Kuenen did not think that this should diminish the possibility of associating these verses with Asherah. He said that the confusion came from a later age, the exilic period, when the redactions were probably being made. It was at this late time that these two deities were being confused with each other, not at the time when Asherah was actually being worshiped.

Thus the text describing the Josian reform shows that Asherah worship included specific Temple rituals demanding utensils and cult personnel. The Canaanite cult had been adopted in large measure by the Israelites.

H. II Kings 23:6

> From the Temple of the Lord he also removed the sacred pole [hā'ăshērāh], to the Kidron Valley, outside Jerusalem; there he had it burned and beaten to dust, which was then scattered over the common graveyard.

Asherah in this verse is a cult object and not a deity. Ringgren and Gray[50] both agree with this assessment. However, they both said that the object clearly is intended to represent the goddess Asherah, the mother-goddess of the Canaanite pantheon.

The Kidron Valley was the location of the common graveyard. Gray[51] noted that the higher slopes of the Valley were used for common Israelite graves. This would have been a convenient and significant spot for the disposition of the ashes of Asherah, convenient because it was near the Valley where they burned the Asherah, and significant because it represented her death.

Comparing verses 4 and 6, one can see that Asherah refers sometimes to the deity and sometimes to her image. Reed[52] said that one could destroy the image of Asherah and in doing so get rid of the goddess herself. But then the converse must also be true, that one could bring sacrifices to the image of Asherah and in doing so pay homage to her. Then he noted that both Asherah and her image were seen to be in the Temple. If what Reed said is true, and it appears to be, then this implies some relationship between Asherah and Yahweh. This fact, then, supports the suggestion already made that the Israelites saw Yahweh and Asherah as divine consorts.

I. II Kings 23:7

> He tore down the apartments of the cult prostitues which were in the Temple of the Lord, and in which the women wove garments for Asherah [lā'ăshērāh].

This is a particularly valuable text. It contains insights into the cult of Asherah which appear nowhere else.

Sexual rites were taking place in the Temple and were related to the cult of Asherah. Patai[53] argued that it is quite appropriate to assume that these ritual performers [*q^e^dēšîm*] were male. He is of the opinion that if they had been both males and females, both the masculine and the feminine forms would have appeared in the Hebrew text. This is not the case. The Hebrew word is masculine. Furthermore, he suggested that having males in this role made sense, given the nature of Asherah as a mother-goddess. For women suffering from childlessness, the sexual services of the male were available under the auspices of the cult of Asherah.

It was probably women who were most interested in the fertility rites of the mother-goddess. Biale[54] observed that this fact also helps explain Ezra's amazingly strong prohibition, in the 5th century, against marrying foreign women, This was a deuteronomistic reform unknown in the early monarchy.

A further note on the *q^e^dēšîm* comes from Fisher[55] who noted that the term is used in Dt 23:18, I Kg 15:12, 22:47, and this text. Its frequent use in the Ras Shamra texts, which he cited extensively, is nearly always associated with the *khn*, the priest of the Canaanite cult, as though the sexual performers were a class of clergy. Given this observation, the argument is substantiated that the sexual performers must therefore have functioned as part of the sacred rituals. The sexual rite was probably viewed as the ritual fulfillment of the Asherah's role, to be a fertile mother.

The word *bāttîm* has been a curiosity for interpreters. One would normally translate it as "apartments," but since the verb used with it is "to weave," and one does not weave an apartment, interpreters have stumbled. The majority of interpreters have given in to the argument of a more convenient translation, changing it to "garments," to agree with the verb. The proponents of this view are, among others, as follows.

Patai suggested that *bāttîm* should be translated "clothes."

> Apart from the question of how can houses be woven, stylistically it is well-nigh impossible that the word "house" should appear three times in one and the same sentence. The Septuagint has "*stōlas*," i.e. garments, for *bātîm*, which may be based on an original *bādîm* , i.e. "linens." The expression "(a person) clothed in linens" (*bādîm*) appears as a standing epithet for a mystical figure in Ezechiel (9:2, 3, 11, etc.) and Daniel (12:6, 7). Thus it may well be that, from time to time, the Asherah statue was dressed in new linens, and that women considered it a pious act to busy themselves with weaving the material for these garments, on looms set up for this purpose in certain chambers in the Temple compound. The weaving of ritual vestments was a woman's task in Babylonian Temples, at Hierapolis in Syria, and in Greece. It seems that also in Ugarit the makers of sacred vestments had a role in the temple ritual.[56]

Reed[57] suggested that the *bāttîm* were either shrines or garments, though he favored garments. He gave evidence of the Greeks draping their images of deities with garments. Gray[58] suggested that this is supported by the existence of an Arabic cognate, *batt* (garment). Murmelstein[59] cited numerous instances from the literature of Egypt and Babylon that verify the contention that there was a custom of weaving clothes for statues of deities.

While these arguments have some foundation, it is undeniable that the lexical stretch is enormous. Clothes are definitely more appropriate for weaving than apartments, but to have a word in a sentence with two different meanings, *bāttîm*, is not as likely as if it had the same meaning. A more likely explanation is that the word *bāttîm* should be translated as it appears, as apartments. A slight correction to the text, the addition of the preposition "in" (*b-*), would help matters considerably. If the word were rendered *bbttym*, "in the apartments," the entire sentence would make better sense. The women were weaving in the apartments. They were weaving things for Asherah in the cultic sexual ritual apartments, which were mentioned in the first part of the verse.

In addition to this suggestion, it is possible to understand the term "weave" in another sense, giving further insight into the situation. De Moor[60] argued that weaving might be a euphemism for sexual intercourse. He noted that in ancient Ugarit neither Astarte (Athtart) nor Anat were represented as the patronesses of the act of intercourse, leaving the possibility that this was the element of Asherah service which was preserved even into the time of the Israelites.

If it is correct that weaving is a euphemism for sexual intercourse, the interpretation of *bāttîm* as apartments is even more reasonable. Instead of saying that the women were weaving in the apartments of the men who performed sexual rituals, now the verse can be rendered as the women engaging in sexual intercourse in the apartments of the men who performed sexual rituals. Since this is the cultic reason that the apartments existed in the first place, i.e., for intercourse, it seems most reasonable that this is how the verse should be interpreted, much more so than straining the words to say that they wove garments there.

This argument would be more substantial if there were direct evidence from Israel or Ugarit of some other instance of the use of weaving as a euphemism for sexual intercourse. No such evidence has been discovered, but this does not necessarily discredit the argument. It is still more plausible than previous explanations.

It is suggested, therefore, that 23:7 be translated as follows:

> He tore down the apartments of the cult prostitutes which were in the Temple of the Lord, in which the women were having intercourse, that is, in the apartments of Asherah.

It could be argued that in this text there is already an adequately designated place, i.e., "in which," and that a second designation of place, "in the apartments," is a bit clumsey. It is somewhat helpful, therefore, to translate the second designation as in apposition to the first. The "of" in "of Asherah" should then be construed to mean "dedicated to," in accordance with the Hebrew preposition, *l-*.

Asherah was the deity under whose auspices sexual rites were performed. Josiah was understandably offended by this practice. His attempt to wipe out the service of Asherah was valiant. He was convinced that, by burning the Asherah images and the ritual apartments, the worship of Asherah would be stopped.

The people of the ancient near east saw a general correspondence between the heavenly world and the earthly world. McCurley[61] recalled a good example of this is the Baal cycle. In the off-season, nature was seen as dead, so Baal was dead. In the sacred rituals, Baal was brought back to life. As a result, the rains would come and life would return to the fields. Since McCurley's recollection is correct, one might suspect that if there was sexual intercourse in the rituals of the Asherah cult, then the people would have seen corresponding activity taking place in the heavenly world. So the question is: with whom did Asherah have intercourse? The answer is simple: with the Lord their God, Yahweh, beside whose altar stood the image of Asherah.

J. II Kings 23:14-15

> 14He broke to pieces the pillars, cut down the sacred poles [hā'ăshērîm], and filled the places where they had been with human bones. 15Likewise the altar which was at Bethel, the high place built by Jeroboam, son of Nebat, who caused Israel to sin—this same altar and high place he tore down, {breaking up the stones and grinding them to powder,} and burning the Asherah [ʾ ăshērāh].[62]

Josiah's purge of Bethel began c621 B.C.E. Eissfeldt[63] noted that Josiah's motive was both national and political, seeking unity and freedom. To this end Josiah emphasized the laws of cultic purity and unity.

The double reference to the high place in verse 15 is best understood if the high place is considered to be the altar itself, or at least the platform on which the altar stood. Vaughan[64] cautioned, however, that there is a double parallel construction which could either support or contend with this interpretation, depending on how it is approached.

In II Kg 23:13, immediately preceding this text, there is reference to Astarte as the Sidonian horror. This, then, is followed by the reference to Asherah. Since Asherah was the goddess of Sidon, this stands as a further example of the confusion between these two deities which arose in the later period, but had not existed in the earlier period of the monarchy.

The place where the Asherah had stood was filled in. This indicates that the upright Asherah post stood in a socket or a hole of some kind. The socket was filled with bones. The human bones could be an allusion to the remnants of the sacrifices, human sacrifices, which had taken place to Mot (Milcom) outside the Temple in the Kidron Valley. The placing of such bones in the socket where the Asherah stood would have been an insult. These bones, representing the horrible and abominable sacrifices, further desecrated the spot where awful Asherah had stood.

The Asherah was, as a cult object, a post which stood erect near the altar, mounted in some kind of socket. Worship of the goddess Asherah was more acceptable to the Yahwists than worship of

Baal, though in the extreme of aberration even Baal was included. Baalist worship was purged more often and with more success than the devout and widespread worship of beloved Asherah. Asherah worship extended throughout the entire historical span of this book.

In the accounts of II Kings, heavily redacted by the deuteronomist, Asherah was revealed as a central cult figure in popular Israelite and Judahite worship. Her cult object occupied a place of honor in the Temple and was found nearly everywhere in the countryside. Devotion to Asherah included various rituals requiring utensils or vessels and engaging the use of males in sexual ritual to impregnate childless women. Furthermore, Asherah was seen, in the popular view, as the divine consort of Yahweh, the Lord, their God.

II Kings showed that there continued a growing confusion between Asherah and Astarte. Their identities were in the process of fusing in the Hebrew cult.

Notes

1 John Gray, *I & II Kings: A Commentary*, 2nd ed. (Philadelphia: Westminster, 1970), pp. 591-92.

2 William L. Reed, *The Asherah in the Old Testament* (Fort Worth: Texas Christian University, 1949), p. 31; and Raphael Patai, *The Hebrew Goddess* (New York: Avon, Discus Book, 1978), pp. 28-9.

3 G. W. Ahlström, *Aspects of Syncretism in Israelite Religion* (Lund: C. W. K. Gleerup, 1963), p. 51.

4 William Foxwell Albright, *The Biblical Period from Abraham to Ezra* (New York: Harper Torchbook, 1963), p. 70.

5 Otto Eissfeldt, *The Old Testament: An Introduction*, trans. P. R. Ackroyd (New York: Harper & Row, 1965), pp. 243, 301.

6 Gray, *I & II Kings*, p. 638.

7 Peter F. Ellis, C.SS.R., "1-2 Kings," in *The Jerome Biblical Commentary*, eds. Raymond E. Brown, et al. (Englewood Cliffs, New Jersey: Prentice Hall, Inc., 1968), p. 204.

8 Reed, *The Asherah*, p. 31.

9 Raphael Patai, "The Goddess Asherah," *Journal of Near Eastern Study* 24 (1965): 47.

10 Reed, *The Asherah*, p. 53.

11 Gray, *I & II Kings*, p. 648.

12 *hāʾăšerôt* is suggested by LXX, Syriac, Hebrew Ms according to B. Kennicott, Targum Ms ed. by Sperber, and the Vulgate.

13 John Bright, *A History of Israel*, 3rd ed. (Philadelphia: Westminster, 1981), p. 282.

14 Yohanan Aharoni, *The Land of the Bible: A Historical Geography*, enlarged ed., trans. and ed. by A. F. Rainey (Philadelphia: Westminster, 1979), p. 379.

15 Jonathan Rosenbaum, "Hezekiah's Reform and Deuteronomistic Tradition," *Harvard Theological Review* 72 (1979): 24.

16 Reed, *The Asherah*, p. 63.

17 Peter Kjeseth, "Nehushtan and Ernst Bloch—Raymond Brown and Biblical Studies," *Dialog* 17 (1978): 281-82.

18 Helmer Ringgren, *Israelite Religion*, trans. David E. Green (Philadelphia: Fortress Press, 1975), p. 148.

19 Patai, *Hebrew Goddess*, p. 35.

20 Karen Randolph Joines, "The Bronze Serpent in the Israelite Cult," *Journal of Biblical Literature* 87 (1968): 253.

21 Joines, "The Bronze Serpent," p. 256. For more on serpents see Kjeseth, "Nehushtan;" Rosenbaum, "Hezekiah's Reform;" and Roger S. Boraas, "Of Serpents and Gods," *Dialog* 17 (1978): 273-79.

22 Roland De Vaux, *The Early History of Israel*, trans. David Smith (Philadelphia: Westminster, 1978), pp. 552-55. Ringgren, *Israelite Religion*, p. 165 also suggested this theory.

23 Saul M. Olyan. *Asherah and the Cult of Yahweh in Israel*, SBL Monograph Series, No. 34, (Atlanta, Georgia: Scholars Press, 1988), pp. 70-71.

24 *ʾašerôt* is suggested by LXX, Syriac, and Vulgate.

25 Reed, *The Asherah*, p. 63; Eissfeldt, *The OT*, p. 243; and Gray, *I & II Kings*, pp. 704-5.

26 Patrick H. Vaughan, *The Meaning of "BAMA" in the Old Testament* (Cambridge, England: Cambridge University Press, 1974), p. 32.

27 Bright, *A History*, p. 312.

28 Ringgren, *Israelite Religion*, p. 99.

29 Patai, "The Goddess Asherah," p. 50.

30 Reed, *The Asherah*, pp. 35-6.

31 J. C. de Moor, "Asherah," in *Theological Dictionary of the Old Testament*, vol. 1, eds. G. Johannes Botterweck and Helmer Ringgren (Grand Rapids: William B. Eerdmans, 1979), pp. 441-2.

32 Helmer Ringgren, *Religions of the Ancient Near East*, trans. John Sturdy (Philadelphia: Westminster, 1973), p. 141.

33 Tadanori Yamashita, *The Goddess Asherah*, a dissertation for Yale University (Ann Arbor: University Microfilms International, 1964), p. 124.

34 Reed, *The Asherah*, p. 50.

35 Gray, *I & II Kings*, p. 707.

36 Edward Lipinski, "The Goddess Atirat in Ancient Arabia, in Babylon, and in Ugarit," *Orientalia Lovaniensia Periodica* 3 (1972): 113.

37 Reed, *The Asherah*, p. 51.

38 Reed, *The Asherah*, p. 56.

39 Von Christoph Dohmen, "Heisst Semel 'Bild, Statue'?" *Zeitschrift für die alttestamentliche Wissenschaft* 96 (1984): 264-65.

40 Aharoni, *The Land*, p. 323.

41 Eissfeldt, *The OT*, p. 297; and Gray, *I & II Kings*, pp. 714-15.

42 Ringgren, *Israelite Religion*, p.211.

43 Michael D. Goulder, *The Psalms of the Sons of Korah*, Journal for the Study of the OT Supplement Series, no. 20 (Sheffield, England: JSOT Press, 1982), p.80.

44 Roland De Vaux, *Ancient Israel*, 2 vols. (New York: McGraw-Hill, 1965), pp. 378-79.

45 Bright, *A History*, pp. 318-19; and Ellis, "1-2 Kings," p. 207.

46 Ahlström, *Aspects of Syncretism*, pp. 74-88.

47 Reed, *The Asherah*, p. 34.

48 M. R. Lehmann, "A New Interpretation of the Term *sdmwt*," *Vetus Testamentum* 3 (1953): 361-71. Gray, *I & II Kings*, p. 732 suggests this theory.

49 James B. Pritchard, *Palestinian Figurines in Relation to Certain Goddesses Known Through Literature*, American Oriental Series, no. 24 (New Haven: American Oriental Society, 1943), p. 62; and A. Kuenen, *The Religion of Israel to the Fall of the Jewish State*, trans. Alfred H. May (London: Williams and Norgate, 1882), p. 90.

50 Ringgren, *Religions of the ANE*, p. 141; and Gray, *I & II Kings*, p. 734.

51 Gray, *I & II Kings*, p. 734.

52 Reed, *The Asherah*, pp. 88, 95.

53 Patai, *The Hebrew Goddess*, p. 283, nt. 56.

54 David Biale, "The God with Breasts: El Shaddai in the Bible," *History of Religions* 20 (1982): 255.

55 Loren Fisher, ed., *Ras Shamra Parallels: The Texts from Ugarit and the Hebrew Bible*, vol. 2, Analecta Orientalia, no. 50 (Rome: Pontifical Biblical Institute, 1975), p. 67.

56 Patai, *The Hebrew Goddess*, p. 283, nt. 56.

57 Reed, *The Asherah*, pp. 51, 88. See also H. Goldman, "The Origin of the Greek Herm," *American Journal of Archaeology* 46 (1942): 61-2.

58 Gray, *I & II Kings*, p. 730, note f.

59 B. Murmelstein, "Spuren altorientalischer Einflüsse im Rabbinschen Schriftum," *Zeitschrift für die alttestamentliche Wissenchaft* 81 (1969): 223. Others who favor this interpretation are Yamashita, *The Goddess*, p. 128 (hangings); De Vaux, *Ancient Israel*, p. 322 (veils); Pritchard, *Palestinian Figurines*, p. 62 (coverings); and Gray, *I & II Kings*, p. 730 (robes).

60 De Moor, "Asherah," p. 441. See also Murmelstein, "Spuren altorientalischer Einflüsse," p. 225.

61 Foster R. McCurley, *Ancient Myths and Biblical Faith: Scriptural Transformations* (Philadelphia: Fortress Press, 1983), p. 89.

62 {---} in LXX is *kaì synétripsen toùs líthous aùtou kaí èléptynen*, which would be Hebrew *way^e šabbēr ʾet ʾ^ă bānāw wayyādeq*, and essentially the same in English: he broke in pieces the stones of it and reduced it to powder. Gray, *I & II Kings*, p. 731 suggests reading *hādēq*, the infinitive absolute, instead of *hēdāq*.

63 Eissfeldt, *the OT*, p. 232.

64 Vaughan, *BAMA*, p. 32.

Chapter 7

II Chronicles[1]

It was a sad fact, but the deuteronomic reforms had failed to take hold. The people of Israel had suffered in the throes of destruction and exile, which the deuteronomistic theologians blamed on the people's failure to follow God's commands. A new approach was needed. The Chronicler, from his post-exilic standpoint, saw the need to arouse concern for the true cult, now being re-established, and a new government which he desired to be a theocracy even though they were dominated by the Persians. So the Chronicler, in the tones of the Priestly tradition of the Pentateuch, emphasized the glory of David as the cultic leader, the supremacy of the southern kingdom as the true Israel, and all the liturgical functions.

The most widely held opinion about the redaction of I and II Chronicles is that it is the work of a single theologian.[2] A newer theory, held principly by some U.S. scholars, is that I and II Chronicles are actually a combination of three separate editions.[3] The original and longest edition, according to them, was I Ch 10 through II Ch 34. Since all of the Chronicles texts considered in this study of Asherah fall within the scope of the supposed original edition, a discussion of the relative value of these two theories is not helpful here, and will not be included.

The date of the Chronicler's work is debated. The usual range of estimates is from the late 6th century to the late 4th century. It may be true that the Chronicler rewrote history from his own theological viewpoint, but his dependence on the deuteronomistic history is obvious. The parallels are numerous and sometimes exact.

It is with this interdependence in mind that the study of the Chronicler's accounts of Asherah proceed.[4]

In the Chronicles it is once again acknowledged that the Asherah was both a cult object, a wooden idol, and the goddess who was represented by the idol. The texts also reaffirm that Asherah worship had been widespread and perduring among the Israelites. All attempts to eliminate her cult ultimately failed. Moreover, there was Asherah worship in the Jerusalem Temple for long periods. The texts will also suggest that Asherah images were not only made of wood, but also made of metal or clay. The Chronicler, like the deuteronomist, registered strong protests against the Asherah cult.

1. The Texts of II Chronicles

A. II Chronicles 14:2

> [1Asa did what was good and pleasing to the Lord, his God,[5]] 2removing the heathen altars and high places, breaking into pieces the sacred pillars, and cutting down the sacred poles [hā'ăshērîm].

Chapters 14 to 16 of Chronicles describe the reign of Asa. Though it parallels Kings, it is obviously greatly expanded. The parallel to II Ch 14:1-7 is I Kg 15:11-12. This particular passage in Kings does not contain any reference to the Asherah, but I Kg 15:13 does verify Asa's act of removing the Asherahs.

The Chronicler has retained the terms used in Kings to describe the foreign cult, i.e., the altars, high places, pillars, and Asherahs. This is an indication that although the Chronicler was rewriting the history which was recorded by the deuteronomist, he did not see fit to alter the mention of these objects. Assuming that he wanted his audience to understand what he wrote, it is a logical conclusion that these particular terms remained understandable to his post-exilic audience. Whether or not Asherah was still worshiped in early post-exilic times is highly debatable, but that her name was remembered is not.

Myers[6] correctly identified the Asherahs in this verse as a reference to the cult object rather than to the goddess herself. The goddess Asherah is, however, implied in any reference to the object bearing her name. Reed[7] noted that *hammanim* (II Ch 14:4, "incense altars") appear near the Asherah four times in the Hebrew Bible, in II Ch 14:4, 34:4-7; Is 17:8, and 27:9. He said the Hebrew Bible does not express the relationship between the two, but does assume that there is one which the audience understands. That relationship may perhaps be explained by artifacts.

B. II Chronicles 15:16

> Maacah, the mother of King Asa, he deposed as queen mother because she had made an outrageous object for Asherah [la'ăshērāh]; Asa cut this down, smashed it, and burned it in the Kidron Valley.

The parallel verses to II Ch 15:16-18 are I Kg 15:13-14. This verse differs from the Kings version especially in that the Asherah is not called an Asherah but an outrageous object. Instead, it is an object set up for Asherah, the goddess. Does this mean that it was not an Asherah object, a wooden post, but some other object? Not necessarily, and probably not. The object named in the Kings version was the wooden post. The Chronicler's version, a euphemistic rewording, does not exclude the fact that it is still the wooden post. Therefore it should be assumed that it is still the post.

Myers[8] said that this horrible object, the *mplst*, was understandably associated with Asherah. The queen mother, Maacah of Tyre, was surely familiar with Asherah since Asherah was the goddess most revered in Tyre.

The LXX translates the Asherah as Astarte. Pritchard[9] observed that this is an example of the fusion of identities which was taking place with these goddesses.

C. II Chronicles 17:6

> Thus he was encouraged to follow the Lord's ways, and again he removed the high places and the sacred poles [hā'ăshērîm] from Judah.

Jehoshaphat continued the kind of reforms that Asa, his father, had begun. The accounts of Kings all but omit mention of Jehoshaphat (I Kg 15:24; II Kg 3:1, 8:16). One ought not speculate too much about why the author(s) of Kings made little mention of Jehoshaphat. But a reason is rather apparent for the Chronicler's choice to include him. The reforms of Jehoshaphat were, at least in part, liturgical. The Chronicler was deeply interested in emphasizing the liturgical connections of the Davidic succession. This, then, a liturgically connected action by a successor of David to the throne of Judah, could not be forgotten.

Jehoshaphat is said to have done exactly what his father did, destroy the Asherahs. The question arises, if Asa had done it, why did Jehoshaphat do it 'again?' Patai[10] suggested two possible explanations. The first is that Asa did not complete the work, so Jehoshaphat was merely continuing where Asa had left off. Considering the widespread use of Asherah in Judah, this explanation seems likely enough. Yet the text about Asa is definitive, giving no indication that Asa's work was incomplete. On the contrary, it implies that Asa was successful in removing the Asherahs. So it is Patai's second explanation that seems more likely: After Asa finished with his bold act of removing all the Asherahs, they sprang up again. Thus the task needed to be repeated by Jehoshaphat. This explanation is attractive. It also indicates the depth of the popular attachment to Asherah, as well as how nearly impossible was the task of trying to abolish Asherah worship.

D. II Chronicles 19:3

> Yet some good things are to be found in you, since you have removed the sacred poles [ha'ăshērôt] from the land and have been determined to seek God.

This verse has no parallel in Kings. Here Jehoshpahat is being addressed by Jehu the seer, who was rebuking Jehoshaphat because of his errors of judgment, while admitting at the same time that there may be hope for Jehoshaphat, for the reason stated in the text. It is a back-handed compliment, to be sure, but a compliment nevertheless.

Asherah is obviously being depicted as a cult object in this text. Reed[11] noted that *bʿr* in its Piel form can mean "to consume, to burn, to remove." The implication of the verse is that if the object is removed, worship of Asherah, the deity it represents, is also removed.

E. II Chronicles 24:18

> They forsook the Temple of the Lord, the God of their fathers, and began to serve the sacred poles [ha'ăshērîm] and idols; and because of this crime of theirs, wrath came upon Judah and Jerusalem.[12]

Chapter 24 has a segment which gives historical additions to the account of Kings, as Myers[13] described. This verse has no parallel in Kings.

King Jehoiadah had been a good and loyal king in the eyes of the Chronicler, worshiping only Yahweh and favoring the Jerusalem cult. His son, Joash, the subject of this text, was the opposite. He was led astray by the princes of Judah (24:17), presumably those who remembered the old ways. He brought back the Canaanite practices. In verses 23-24 Joash was punished by the invasion of the Syrians. It appears that the punishment was due to his sin as recorded in 24:18.

This text is in parallel form, containing two similar words, yet the meanings are different enough to warrant using two separate words to describe them. Reed[14] noted that the idols in this verse come from the root *ʿaṣab*, and should thus be translated literally as "the things which are formed." The verse implies that the Asherah is an idol, but that it is not exactly the same as other idols. Perhaps the only difference is that it is simply one kind of idol. Reed also suggested that the use of *ʿebed* here implies that a cultic ritual akin to sacrifice was taking place before the Asherah.

There is no mention of a specific time when the Asherah was reintroduced into the Temple. Patai[15] suggested that it happened at this time, and that it remained there until Hezekiah removed it 100 years later.

Pritchard[16] noted that here again the Asherah is translated as Astarte in the LXX. He described this phenomenon as a strong indication that Asherah and Astarte were being confused with each other by the time of the LXX translation.

This verse, then, suggests that, in the memory of the Chronicler and his sources, the Asherah had been a particular kind of idol and that some kind of sacrificial rites had taken place in the Asherah cult.

F. II Chronicles 31:1

> After all this was over, those Israelites who had been present went forth to the cities of Judah and smashed the sacred pillars, cut down the sacred poles [ha'ăshērîm], and tore down the high places and altars throughout Judah, Benjamin, Ephraim, Manasseh, until all were destroyed.

The territories mentioned in this text give a geographical idea of the extent of Asherah worship. Benjamin and Manasseh were both located at the northernmost segment of the Israelite territory, and Judah was the southernmost province. The intent here is clearly to say that Asherah worship was everywhere. Since these geographical locations were not mentioned in the parallel text in Kings, and since the Chronicler perhaps did not have direct experience of the Asherah cult, one might suspect that the description of Asherah worship as being so widespread might be more due to the Chronicler's zeal than to his verifiable knowledge. Ironically, though, the Chronicler was correct, since II Kings demonstrates clearly that Asherah worship was, in fact, widespread.

The parallel of this verse in Kings is II Kings 18:4. The Chronicler presented Hezekiah as a second David. Myers[17] noted that the reforms of Hezekiah were an act of re-centralization, the kind of centralizing that David first accomplished. He noted that this account is greatly expanded from the Kings account, and has a strong emphasis on Levitical matters as well as the specifically cultic aspects of the Davidic heritage.

The mention of Nehushtan is absent from the Chronicler's rendering of this history. Rosenbaum[18] suggested two reasons for this history. First is the possibility that the Chronicler was using a non-deuteronomic source for his history of this period. The second, more defensible, regards the theological bias of the Chronicler. The Chronicler favored the Aaronite priesthood over the Mosaic priesthood. It would be understandable if he omitted the reference to Nehusthan, which was associated directly with Moses.

Immediately preceding this text is the account of a festival. Rosenbaum[19] noted that the act of centralizing the cult and the nation, as well as the act of destroying the abominations, grew naturally from the celebration of the festival. This is a markedly liturgical interpretation of history. It also shows that the acts represented in 31:1 were the crux of Hezekiah's reform, including the eradication of Asherahs from the land.

G. II Chronicles 33:3

> He rebuilt the high places which his father Hezekiah had torn down, erected altars for the Baals, made sacred poles [ha'ăshērôt], and postrated himself before the whole host of heaven and worshiped them.

Chapter 33 is the struggle of the Chronicler to explain how Manasseh could have reigned so long in spite of his sins. Myers[20] noted that this verse is a declaration of Manasseh's sins. The reforms of Hezekiah, in spite of their depth, were short-lived. His successor, Manasseh, brought back all the foreign ways in full force.

Asherah is plural in this verse, whereas in its parallel in II Kg 21:3 it is singular. This is easily explained by the Chronicler's desire to emphasize the re-centralization of the cult. This was more aptly described with many Asherahs being eliminated rather than just one.

The word *semel* (image) appears in the Hebrew in verses 7 and 15. This is most likely a reference to the Asherah. Myers[21] supported this agrument by noting that the parallel verse of this text, II Kg 21:7, mentions Asherah explicitly. Reed[22] saw a possible relationship between the *semel* in 33:7 and Ez 8:4-5, "the statue of jealousy."

This verse shows how Manasseh reintroduced the Asherah cult, probably at popular demand. It spread widely as though it had never really left.

H. II Chronicles 33:19

> His prayer and how his supplication was heard, all his sins and his infidelity, the sites where he built high places and erected sacred poles [ha'ăshērîm] and carved images before he humbled him self, all can be found written down in the history of his seers.

The parallel to this text is II Kings 21:17-18. This verse, as suggested within the verse itself, is derived from a historical source which no longer exists, the history of the seers. Myers[23] suggested that it was originally recorded as a separate document and later copied into this book. Eissfeldt[24] was less daring. He said that the text can show only that the writings of the prophets are parts of the books of Samuel and Kings and the Midrash based upon them.

Reed[25] noted that the verb used with Asherah is *ʿmd*. It is in the Hiphil here, so that it is best translated as "set up, erect."

This verse summarizes the aberrations of Manasseh with harsh tones of condemnation, yet allowed that even he could be forgiven when he repented.

I. II Chronicles 34:3, 4, and 7

> 3In the eighth year of his reign, while he was still a youth, he began to seek after the God of his forefather David, and in his twelfth year he began to purge Judah and Jerusalem of the high places, the sacred poles [ha'ăshērîm], and the carved and molten images. 4In his presence the altars of the Baals were destroyed; the incense stands erected above them were torn down; the sacred poles [ha'ăshērîm] and the carved and molten images were shattered and beaten into dust, which was strewn over the tombs of those who had sacrificed to them. He destroyed the altars, broke up the sacred poles [ha'ăshērîm] and carved images and beat them into dust, and tore down the incense stands throughout the land of Israel. Then he returned to Jerusalem.

Chapters 34-35 are largely parallel to II Kings, chapters 12-13, although the Chronicler's version is expanded with some non-deuteronomistic material. Myers[26] described the Davidic reference in 34:3 as typical of the Chronicler's expansions. Verses 3, 4, and 7 have no direct parallel in the Kings version, although they seem at least indirectly sympathetic to II Kg 23:4-20.

Josiah's reform began in 633 B.C.E., the year of Ashurbanipal's death. According to Aharoni[27], this is sensible, because his reform was surely an act of rebellion against Assyria. The death of Assyria's leader would have thrown Assyria into disarray, such that the time would be ripe for rebellion in the distant provinces of Palestine. Aharoni also suggested that Josiah's ritual purification of Judah and Israel began in 629 B.C.E., the year after the death of Ashurbanipal's son and successor, Ashur-etil-ilani. Bright and North[28] agreed with these dates. Eissfeldt[29] also agreed with them, but more cautiously. He said that one must withhold any attempts to fully reconstruct the course of these events.

North[30] noted that there is no longer any mention of Assyrian cult figures, i.e., the host of heaven, but now only Canaanite cult figures. Although he offered no explanation, the reason is simple. Now that Assyria no longer dominated Palestine, there was no need to continue the official cult of their deities. The host of heaven was no longer an imposing threat to Yahwism. The threat was now focused on the real enemies: Baal and Asherah.

Verse 34:4 mentions "carved and molten images" for the first time with Asherah. This gives rise to a new possibility, that not only were the Asherahs found in high places, but that they were available in metal, wood, or even clay forms for general use, bringing to mind "upon every high hill and under every green tree" from I Kg 14:23.

Reed[31] observed that the verbs used in 34:4-7 to describe the destruction of the Asherah were very strong verbs: *sbr* (to break into pieces), *nt̩s* (to overturn), *dqq* (to grind to dust). This shows the Chronicler's desire to convey the zeal of Josiah. It also shows the Chronicler's own strong reaction to the Asherah cult.

Noticing the phrase "throughout the land of Israel" in 34:7, Aharoni[32] suggested that it implies an extensive area under the control of Josiah. If so, it also implies an extensive area which needed purging of Asherahs.

In a note on the texts of 15:8-15 and 29, Myers[33] said that in spite of their similarity with 34:3-7, the pattern here should be treated as an accurate account of its own. Apparently the same purging needed to take place over and over again.

This passage has shown that the Chronicler considered Asherah a threat to Yahwism. Asherah images proliferated everywhere, some made of wood, others of metal or clay. The Chronicler heartily endorsed Josiah's attempt to rid the nation of Asherah worship.

The Chronicler wrote a revisionist history based on the earlier deuteronomic history and was theologically biased toward the cultic role of the Davidic kingship in Judah. Since many of these texts of Chronicles, as listed above, have their parallels in Kings (14:2, 15:16, 31:1, 33:3, 33:19, and 34:3-7), many comments would be repetitions, and therefore are left presumed from the previous chapter.

The Chronicler remembered the Canaanite cult objects and deities found in Kings, including the Asherah. So did his audience of the post-exilic era. References are both to the goddess Asherah and to her cult object(s). She appears now to have some relationship not only to the wooden post, but to the smaller figurines ("images") and the incense altars. Her manner of presence with the cult objects was suggested to be such that if the objects were destroyed, so was her cult. Some kind of sacrifices were offered in the sanctuary in relation to her cult object.

Asherah worship was extensive in the Chronicler's historical scope, from north to south in the territories of Israel and Judah. It was also extremely difficult to eradicate. Regular reforms and purges gained only temporary diminishment of Asherah worship. It was never fully eliminated. It remained an important element in the popular religion of the followers of Yahweh.

With the passing of Assyria as a dominating force, so passed the Assyrian deities from Israel and Judah. This left the people free and able to focus on the local Canaanite deities, such as Asherah, to whom they were devoted. The Chronicler lamented this devotion.

Finally, the Chronicler brought to mind a situation that was developing at least by his time. There continued the confusion between Asherah and Astarte, especially from the time of the translation of the LXX. Asherah was becoming fused with Astarte, and their names were being interchanged.

Notes

1 For various reasons the Chronicler's accounts have attracted the attention of most biblical historians, but few textual interpreters.

A fair amount of what is reported by the Chronicler was also reported in the deuteronomic histories. Repetition of comments will be avoided in this study as much as possible.

2 Martin Noth, *Überlieferungsgeschichtliche Studien I* (Tübingen: M. Niemeyer, 1957), pp. 110-123.

3 F. M. Cross, "A Reconstruction of the Judean Restoration," *Journal of Biblical Literature* 94 (1975): 4-18.

4 For more introductory materials to Chronicles, see William Sanford La Sor, et al., *Old Testament Survey: The Message, Form, and Background of the Old Testament* (Grand Rapids: William B. Eerdmans, 1982); Otto Eissfeldt, *The Old Testament: An Introduction*, trans P. R. Ackroyd (New York: Harper & Row, 1965); and Jacob M. Myers, *II Chronicles*, Anchor Bible, vol. 13 (New York: Doubleday & Co., 1965).

5 The LXX appends this verse to the end of chapter 13. The English is numbered according to the Hebrew.

6 Myers, *II Chronicles*, p. 83.

7 William L. Reed, *The Asherah in the Old Testament* (Fort Worth: Texas Christian University, 1949), p. 51.

8 Myers, *II Chronicles*, p. 89.

9 James B. Pritchard, *Palestinian Figurines in Relation to Certain Godesses Known Through Literature*, American Oriental Series, no. 24 (New Haven: American Oriental Society, 1943), p. 62.

10 Raphael Patai, *The Hebrew Goddess* (New York: Avon, Discus Book, 1978), p. 34.

11 Reed, *The Asherah*, p. 35.

12 *b^erît* is suggested for *bêt* in LXX, Syriac, and the Kennicott Heb. Ms.

13 Myers, *II Chronicles*, p. lix.

14 Reed, *The Asherah*, p. 52.

15 Raphael Patai, "The Goddess Asherah," *Journal of Near Eastern Study* 24 (1965): 49.

16 Pritchard, *Palestinian Figurines*, p. 63.

17 Myers, *II Chronicles*, pp. lx, 183.

18 Jonathan Rosenbaum, "Hezekiah's Reform and Deuteronomistic Tradition," *Harvard Theological Review* 72 (1979): 36-7.

19 Rosenbaum, "Hezekiah's Reform," p. 38.

20 Myers, *II Chronicles*, p. lx.

21 Myers, *II Chronicles*, p. 197.

22 Reed, *The Asherah*, p. 92.

23 Myers, *II Chronicles*, p. xlvii.

24 Eissfeldt, *The OT*, p. 534.

25 Reed, *The Asherah*, p. 31.

26 Myers, *II Chronicles*, p. lxi.

27 Yohanan Aharoni, *The Land of the Bible: A Historical Geography*, rev. and enlarged ed., trans. and ed. by A. F. Rainey (Philadelphia: Westminster, 1979), p. 401.

28 John Bright, *A History of Israel*, 3rd ed. (Philadelphia: Westminster, 1981), p. 318; and Robert North, S.J., "The Chronicler: 1-2 Chronicles, Ezra, Nehemiah," in *The Jerome Biblical Commentary*, eds. Raymond E. Brown, et al. (Englewood Cliffs, New Jersey: Prentice Hall, Inc., 1968), p. 425.

29 Eissfeldt, *The OT*, p. 536.

30 North, "The Chronicler," p. 425.

31 Reed, *The Asherah*, p. 35.

32 Aharoni, *The Land*, p. 404.

33 Myers, *II Chronicles*, p. 205.

Chapter 8

Isaiah, Jeremiah, and Micah

The four Asherah texts in the prophetic literature affirm the influence of Asherah worship in the Hebrew cult. Isaiah, offended by the worship of foreign deities, warned his audience that the foreign cults were off limits. The text's editor added Asherah to the list of offenses in both Isaiah passages, showing his revulsion to Asherah worship. Jeremiah and Micah joined the deuteronomistic editor in leveling scathing criticism against the Asherah cult among the Israelites.

1. The Prophetic Texts

A. Isaiah 17:8

> He shall not look to the altars, his handiwork, nor shall he regard what his fingers have made: the sacred poles or the incense stands.

This text and the following one are found in First Isaiah, the preexilic complaints. They both appear in a large section, chapters 13 to 23, which contains the oracles against the foreign nations. The occasion of this text is an oracle against Damascus. The antecedent of the initial "he," however, is not Damascus, but all humanity, hence the RSV "they." The prophet is describing what will happen to all humanity, especially the Chosen People, on the day Damascus falls.

There is a problem with this text. While it is part of a genuine Isaian segment, the references to Asherah appears to be a gloss. Eissfeldt[1] described this text as part of a collection of genuine Isaian sayings which were assembled during the Assyrian period.

More specifically, Moriarty[2] dated this oracle $_c$734 B.C.E., shortly before Tiglath-Pileser III conquered Damascus. The threats against Israel in this oracle are because Israel was allied with Aram, whose capital was Damascus. This alliance threatened Judah. The poles, Moriarty said, refer to the goddess Asherah.

The final phrases about the sacred poles and the incense stands is a gloss by a later editor, noted Kaiser, inspired to make a parallel with 17:10 by providing specific details. Elliger and Rudolph[3] supported this suggestion. A further argument for this is the fact that Is 2:8 is also parallel to this. When one attempts to determine which of two verses is earlier, usually the shorter is earlier than the longer. So it is in this case. The composition of 2:8 precedes 17:8, making 17:8 the more likely candidate to be considered a gloss. This could be considered a timely gloss, not an intrusion into history or an anacronism, in the sense that it accurately reflects the events of an age for which there are extensive arguments that Asherah was being worshiped.

The association here of the Asherah and the incense stand is not described, but there does appear to be some relationship between them. Implied in this passage is an attitude that the Asherah was offensive to the prophet, just as a foreign incense stand would offend him. The prophet expected his listeners to be warned that their clinging to foreign cult worship of Asherah would cost them dearly. The prophetic redactor, a conservative like the prophet, remained steadfast in opposing all cultic aberrations, including the Asherah.

B. Isaiah 27:9

> This, then, shall be the expiation of Jacob's guilt, this the whole fruit of the removal of his sin: he shall pulverize all the stones of the altars like pieces of chalk; no sacred poles ['ăshērîm] or incense stands shall stand.

This passage explains that the people's sin could not be forgiven until they removed the foreign cult, including Asherah worship, from their midst. While it may not be a genuine Isaian passage, it nevertheless reflects his editor's strong conviction that Asherah worship was wrong.

It was not suffering which was the prerequisite for the expiation of sin, but the elimination of the foreign cult, as Patai[4] noted. The intended date, however, was the indeterminate future, not Isaiah's own era.

Some scholars insist that this text is a gloss. Moriarty and Eissfeldt[5] considered this text a miscellaneous fragment. Eissfeldt was especially harsh, saying that all of chapters 24-27 are entirely inauthentic, and that this particular passage, verses 2-11, is a reflective text which has no literary link with its context. He said that it is one of four songs of thanksgiving (24:7-16a, 25:1-5, 26:1-14, and 27:2-11) which are all additions.

Other scholars work with the text under the assumption that it is not a gloss. Kaiser[6] made no suggestion at all that this text might be a gloss. He called this verse a prophecy looking toward the future. He described the Asherah here as the cult object, the standing wooden pillar referred to in Jg 6:25 and Dt 12:3. Reed[7] noted that *yāqumû*, from *qūm*, can be translated as "stand" or "rise".

If the claims are true that this passage is not genuinely Isaian, and this seems to be the case, then it was not Isaiah but his editor who was concerned with the effects of the presence of Asherah worship in Judah. This text is, obviously, at least indirectly associated with the deuteronomic tradition. In either case, there was sufficient worry to include it in such a way that Judah would understand that eliminating Asherah worship and the rest of the Canaanite cult would result in the expiation of their sins.

C. Jeremiah 17:2

> 1The sin of Judah is written...2when their sons remember their altars and their sacred poles [wa'ăshērêhem], beside the green trees, on the high hills.

This passage can be dated 605-603, as explained by Couturier[8], during the reign of Jehoiachim in Judah, shortly after Josiah, whose reign ended in 609. Jehoiachim had gone back to the old foreign ways, in spite of the great reforms of his father. The context of this verse is one of Jeremiah's prophecies against his own people.

This text is a genuine but small Jeremian text (17:1-11). Eissfeldt[9] showed this and noted that it was assembled with some other small passages by a later editor.

Jeremiah never mentioned Astarte, observed Patai,[10] but he did mention Baal and the Baal cult many times (2:8, 23; 7:9; 9:13; 11:13, 17; 12:16; 19:5; etc.). One might add to Patai's note, saying that Jeremiah did, however, mention Asherah in this text with the objection that worship of the Asherah was sinful, and that it was widespread. Jeremiah's words bring to mind II Kg 17:10 which attest that Asherahs were found nearly everywhere, and Dt 12:2. This connects Jeremiah with the deuteronomic traditon of decrying Asherah worship.

This text, therefore, shows a Jeremian awareness of the problem of Asherah worship. Jeremiah spoke harshly to his own people, telling them that their involvement with the foreign cult was sinful.

D. Micah 5:13

> 12I will abolish your carved images and the sacred pillars from your midst; and you shall no longer adore the works of your hands. 13I will tear out the sacred poles ['ăshêreyka] from your midst, and destroy your cities.

Micah prophesied in the last quarter of the 8th century, ending after Hezekiah began his reforms. One might suspect that Micah was at least inspired and heartened by the reform, and perhaps was a contributor to the reform movement. Bright[11] placed this section (Mi 5:12-14) in a time contemporary with Ahaz, the predecessor of Hezekiah. Under Ahaz idolatrous practices flourished.

Reflecting the trend of modern scholarship, Mays[12] made the claim that this segment is not original to Micah, but came into his collection in the tradition of Isaiah and Hosea (Is 2:6-8, Hos 14:3). He said that it is not typical of Micah to have seen God as the one who will remove the foreign objects, because for Micah it is usually God who punishes those who use them, rather than himself being the agent of change.

In a minority opinion, Eissfeldt[13] replied to the charge of Mays by suggesting that while Micah might resemble Is 2:6-8, he did not copy directly. He transformed the original text into his own. It is known that Micah lived at the same time as Isaiah. Micah's village was a short distance from Jerusalem. It is therefore not only possible but is likely that Micah heard what Isaiah was saying, and perhaps heard him in person. Hillers[14] agreed that this is an authentic passage, arguing that it is congruent with the times of Hezekiah and with the situation of Micah in Judah.

The Micah text has a future orientation. Patai[15] noted that Micah was expecting that the removal of the abominations would take place in a future day. Thus, as Eissfeldt[16] said, the text contains a promise for Israel along with the threat. The elimination of the foreign cult will be a prelude to the new age.

Commentators disagree on how Asherah should be interpreted in this verse. King and Hillers[17] said that the reference to Asherah in this verse was to her cult object, the wooden post. Reed[18] noted that the verb *ntš* can be translated "plucked up, uproot" as well as "tear out." It is the opposite of *nṭ*ᶜ (to plant), but it is also used with objects which have no actual roots, such as cities (Ps 9:7), kingdoms (Dan 11:4), and people (I Kg 14:15). De Moor[19] also admits the possibility of this wider translation, in spite of the possible reference to a plant (*ᶜareykā*) in the next clause. Perhaps this disagreement can be resolved by noting that the Asherahs in this text are in close conjunction with other cult objects, the carved images and pillars. This association turns the argument in favor of those who say that the Asherahs are cult objects, not cities.

The texts of Isaiah, Jeremiah, and Micah spoke against the cultic practice of honoring the cult object of Asherah, the wooden post. It appears to be the same widespread cult as appeared in other parts of the Hebrew Bible. The prophetic references to Asherah seem to be congruent with those of the deuteronomic tradition.

There are only four prophetic texts which mention Asherah. Among these few, only one is authentic to the prophets themselves. Why would the prophets, so many of whom prophesied during the monarchy when Asherah worship flourished, have neglected to speak against her? One possibility is that her cult was not as widespread or noticeable as the deuteronomistic redactor or the Chronicler would have us believe. Another is that they were not so much bothered by Asherah worship as the other abuses against which they railed. Perhaps they thought that, compared to social injustice and political corruption, the worship of Asherah was not a serious problem. A third possibility is that the prophetic redactors, many of whom were not deuteronomistic, had no particular need to speak against Asherah worship, and therefore did not include the name Asherah in their redactions, even if it might have appeared in the original prophetic sayings. II Isaiah, for example, makes regular mention of idol worship, but never specifically mentions Asherah.

Notes

1 Otto Eissfeldt, *The Old Testament: An Introduction*, trans. P. R. Ackroyd (New York: Harper & Row, 1965), p. 307.

2 Frederick L. Moriarty, S.J., "Isaiah 1-39," in *The Jerome Biblical Commentary*, eds. Raymond E. Brown, et al. (Englewood Cliffs, New Jersey: Prentice Hall, Inc., 1968), p. 275.

3 Otto Kaiser, *Isaiah 13-39: A Commentary* (Philadelphia: Westminster, 1974), p. 83; and *Biblia Hebraeica Stuttgartensia*, eds. K. Elliger and W. Rudolph, vol. 7, "Liber Jesaiae," praep. D. Winton Thomas (Stuttgart: Württembergisch Bibelansstalt, 1968), p. 26.

4 Raphael Patai, *The Hebrew Goddess* (New York: Avon, Discus Book, 1978), p. 35.

5 Moriarty, "Isaiah 1-39," p. 277; and Eissfeldt, *The OT*, pp. 307, 324.

6 Kaiser, *Isaiah 13-39*, p. 228.

7 William L. Reed, *The Asherah in the Old Testament* (Fort Worth: Texas Christian University, 1949), p. 32.

8 Guz P. Couturier, C.S.C., "Jeremiah," in *The Jerome Biblical Commentary*, eds. Raymond E. Brown, et al. (Englewood Cliffs, New Jersey: Prentice Hall, Inc., 1968), p. 302.

9 Eissfeldt, *The OT*, p. 357.

10 Patai, *The Hebrew Goddess*, p. 38.

11 John Bright, *A History of Israel*, 3rd. ed. (Philadelphia: Westminster, 1981), p. 277.

12 James Luther Mays, *Micah: A Commentary* (Philadelphia: Westminster, 1976), pp. 124-25, 127.

13 Eissfeldt, *The OT*, p. 411.

14 Hillers, Delbert R., *Micah*, eds. Paul D. Hanson and Loren Fisher, Hermeneia series (Philadelphia: Fortress Press, 1984), p. 74.

15 Patai, *The Hebrew Goddess*, p. 35.

16 Eissfeldt, *The OT*, p. 408.

17 Phillip J. King, "Micah," in *The Jerome Biblical Commentary*, eds. Raymond E. Brown, et al. (Englewood Cliffs, New Jersey: Prentice Hall, Inc., 1968), pp. 287-88; and Hillers, *Micah*, p. 73.

18 Reed, *The Asherah*, p. 36.

19 J. C. de Moor, "Asherah," in *Theological Dictionary of the Old Testament*, vol. 1, eds. G. Johannes Botterweck and Helmer Ringgren (Grand Rapids: William B. Eerdmans, 1979), p. 442.

PART III

ARCHAEOLOGICAL FACTORS

The world is quite familiar with mother-goddess figurines and drawings. For thousands of years they have been produced by many cultures. This fact makes the identification of particular goddess representations somewhat difficult. Moreover, the fluidity of the characteristics and even names of various similar goddesses makes the identification of their images even more problematic. Inscriptions help a great deal, and it is unfortunate that they are so few in number. Nevertheless, it is encouraging for this study that recent archaeology suggests that the worship of Asherah was common during the monarchic period of Israel.

The Canaanite culture, in the midst of which Israel came to be, was already rather well established by the beginning of the second millennium B.C.E. It was originally an amalgamation of the civilization which grew up around the territory of Byblos and that of the nomads who wandered in the area. Their economic, territorial, and cultic patterns were already a matter of common agreement by c2000 B.C.E.[1] Kathleen Kenyon stated that this culture stretched from Ras Shamra in the north to the Negeb in the south, considering the pottery and equipment which has been discovered in this territory from this period. This is the land in which the ancestors of Israel wandered and where their descendants settled. She noted further that there is evidence that powerful alien rulers came to this territory and took over towns by force, yet the Canaanite culture endured in those same towns. Roving bands, for example the Habiru of the Amarna letters (1390-1365), settled in Canaan, but it was the Canaanite culture which inevitably dominated them. They were absorbed into Canaan, adopting its cult and culture.[2]

Before the Hebrews became a nation of their own, they had become a part of Canaan. It is in this context that the nation of Israel was born. The specific time and mode of this process of Israelite nationalization will be left to other studies, except for the following general comments.

Several suggestions have been made regarding the nature of the nationalization process of Israel. Albright[3] suggested the conquest model, in which Israel is said to have conquered the inner territories of Canaan by military force and occupied them.

Alt, Noth[4], and others espoused an immigration model, in which Israelites peacefully migrated into and settled the inner Canaanite territories. A third model was suggested by Mendenhall and endorsed by Gottwald[5], and is gaining the increasing favor of the scholarly community. It might be called a model of social revolution, in which the origins of Israel did not come from outside the territory, that is, were not by means of conquest or migration, but rather were the result of a religious ideological revolt supported mainly by indigenous peasants.

By whatever means, it is indisputable that the Israelites became the chief rulers in the territories of Israel and Judah, displacing whatever control had originally been held over those territories by the Canaanites. Yet it must be remembered that the Israelites, no matter what their origin and no matter who was in power, lived for a long time in the Canaanite territories, alongside of Canaanite cult and culture. One must expect that they did as the Habiru and others had done, that is allow themselves to be absorbed into the life of Canaan. They adopted, and in some cases adapted, the language, literature, economy, architecture, and cultic practices of Canaan.[6]

Chapters 9 and 10 are a record of Asherah-related archaeological discoveries. The figurines, reliefs, and inscriptions discussed vary in the degrees of certainty with which they can be identified with Asherah. The reports are arranged in approximately chronological order, demonstrating that there is a geographical shift inland of Asherah worship, which corresponds to the rise in power of the inland people, the Israelites. The shift is from the older Canaanite coastal centers to the later Hebrew hill country, where the Israelites were maintaining their monarchy.

Chapter 9

Artifacts

1. Figurines

There are two major studies which have been of special value in this area. The first is by Ora Negbi[7], a study of datable metal votive idols discovered at archaeological excavations. Negbi charted the locations and dates of various types of female statues. One can easily note the geographical shift inland of the distribution of the figurines, beginning from the coastal areas like Ras Shamra in the Middle Bronze Age, and spreading to the inland areas like Megiddo and Gezer in the Late Bronze Age. Negbi rarely identifies any of these statues with any particular deity, because that task was being outside the scope of such a study. Nevertheless there is some hope of providing identifications by other means which will be engaged below. Of special interest will be the Qudshu group, many of which are apparent Asherah representations. Moreover, some of the divine couples, that is male and female deities found as figurines together, appear to contain Asherah as the female element.

Another relevant major study was conducted by James R. Engle.[8] He catalogued a number of terracotta statues according to eye shape, noting their characteristics: ten to twenty cm. high, molded, fine head features and crude body features, exaggerated breasts, short hair, bell-bottomed base, whitewash evidence, lack of jewelry and ornaments, and lack of female physiology below the waist. About a dozen have been found in complete form, and 187 are in partial form, mostly with the bodies broken away and lost.

One type was found almost exclusively at sites in Judah, another at sites almost exclusively outside of Judah to the north and the east, but all within Canaanite territories. He suggested that, though the figurines are all very similar in style, the variance in detail can be attributed simply to more than one place of manufacture. These figurines can be dated from the ninth century to the early sixth, and there is the possibility that they were in existence as early as the Davidic monarchy. While about a quarter of the figurines were found at domestic sites, suggesting that they had a domestic function, others have been found at sites which show clearly their cultic use, sites such as burial places and cultic disposal locations.

Engle was aware that a number of scholars have considered these figurines to be representations of Astarte or have refused to identify them at all.[9] Yet he argued that they are most probably Asherah statues. His argument is as follows. After examining the texts of the Hebrew Scriptures, he saw the need to posit the existence of figurines representing the goddess Asherah, especially when the term used is *asherim*, e.g., I Kg 14:23. Then he examined the various corroborating inscriptions which demonstrate that Asherah was most definitely a deity of Iron Age Israel. Next he noted that in their contemporary Greco-Aegean world such kinds of statuettes were often miniature replicas of a larger "official" statue in the main cultic temple.[10]

Since the seafaring Canaanites were a part of this Greco-Aegean world, one presumes that they knew about this custom of creating replicas of the official cult statue, perhaps as charms, remembrances, or religious tokens. The small statues are themselves evidence that they knew and practiced this custom, at least in a modified fashion. The next step is to conclude that these figurines represent the goddess Asherah. While the weight of the evidence leans in this direction, there is nevertheless no direct evidence to tie the figurines to Asherah. This is unfortunately typical of archaeological arguments, that one can produce probabilities more frequently than certainties.

2. Sites and Artifacts

What follows is a roughly chronological list of archaeological sites excavated in the area of Palestine where Asherah-related artifacts of varying degrees of identifiability have been discovered.

A. Gezer

Gezer is an ancient Canaanite city between Jerusalem and the sea coast. This site has been excavated by such renowned archaeologists as R. A. S. Macalaster, G. E. Wright, Y. Yadin, and W. G. Dever, with further work at the Hebrew Union College. Its strata from the Bronze Age to the Roman era are clearly distinguishable. An Amorite sanctuary from $_c$2000 was unearthed there. Gray[11] reported that there are visible between eight and eleven stone pillars erected in a crescent pattern. In front of two of them are large limestone blocks into which there is cut in each a depression measuring 2'10" by 1'11" by 1'4" deep. Since there is no sign of the protective plaster lining usually put as waterproofing into limestone basins that are to be used to contain liquid, it is suggested that these were not basins, but sockets. Given that stone pillars in Canaan were nearly always symbols of El or Baal, and given that Asherah is the goddess who is most often paired with both of them, and given that the wooden post which represents Asherah is a regular companion to the stone pillar, it is possible that these sockets were meant to support wooden representations of the goddess Asherah. Moreover, Negbi concluded that only one deity was worshiped at Gezer during the Middle Bronze period, a fertility goddess, considering the fact that no figurines have been discovered in its excavated sites except female figurines.[12]

B. Ras Shamra

Ras Shamra, on the north shore of the Palestinian coast of the Mediterranean Sea, 25 miles south of the Orontes River, is the site of ancient Ugarit, which was a flourishing civilized center by 2000 and was a major center of economic and cultural influence till its destruction $_c$1200. It was accidentally discovered in 1928 by C. F.

M. Schaeffer and excavated between 1929 and 1960, also by Schaeffer. This shipping center, being Canaanite, owed its cultural origins not so much to the primitive inhabitants of the surrounding Palestinian areas, but more to the seafaring culture of ancient Byblos. Ugarit, with its port city located nearby at Minet el-Beida, had access to sea commerce in the whole Mediterranean. Its shipping market was concentrated especially in an area marked by Greece in the north and Eygpt in the south, and land commerce into Mesopotamia. Ugarit superimposed its cult and culture on most of Palestine during the years of its existence.[13]

At Ras Shamra there have been discovered archaeological riches that exceed the dreams of most archaeologists. Among them are a palace and two tripartite temples, one dedicated to Baal $_{c}$2000 and another earlier one dedicated to Dagon, both of which are similar to the tripartite temple structure of Solomon's temple in Jerusalem. Also discovered were a huge library of cultic literature and civil records, including a trilingual wordlist which has greatly simplified translation, and many artifacts.

The female goddess figurines found at Ras Shamra rarely bear any kind of distinguishing features, and since several goddesses had notable places in their pantheon, it is therefore not possible to identify these figurines with any particular goddess. However, there are other depictions besides figurines, some of which are identifiable with Asherah. Barrois referred to a pendant which depicts a goddess crossed by two serpents and accompanied by a lion. The lion, in light of its association with Asherah and her counterparts (see Chapters 1 and 2), suggests that she might be Asherah.[14]

An ivory bas relief $_{c}$1300 was discovered on the royal bed in the palace of Ras Shamra.[15] On it there is a panel depicting a goddess nursing two boys. Since Asherah is the mother-goddess, one suspects right away that this might be her image, but the two boys need to be explained. Asherah is known from the Baal epics to have nursed not only gods but also certain extraordinary men. Gray[16] suggested that Asherah nursing a boy would be especially appropriate if one remembers the story of King Keret, whose heir,

Yasab, was singled out above ordinary mortals for suckling by the goddess. Since the goddess to which Keret prayed was Asherah, one might easily suppose that the goddess to do the suckling was also Asherah. The fact that there are two boys, not one, has been explained by Schaeffer as a simple duplication for the sake of artistic symmetry.[17] One could also imagine that any successor to King Yasab who might have commissioned such a work for his royal bed would want to see himself next to the famous Yasab, being suckled by Asherah. He might, therefore, have commanded the royal artist to represent himself on the ivory with Yasab instead of Yasab alone. This suggestion is without a doubt hypothetical, and should not be given any more credence than speculation deserves. Yet the idea is attractive enough to include, hoping that evidence might one day either support or refute it.

An ivory lid to an unguent box was discovered at Ugarit's harbor, Minet el-Beida, from $_{c}$1300.[18] On the ivory is carved a relief in the Mycenean style. It depicts a goddess in Cretan dress and features, taking the place of the usual tree between two caprids rampant, to whom she is offering ears of corn. The tree of life was rather common in palace architecture. It can be found on columns in the Canaanite royal palaces of Jerusalem, Samaria, Hazor, and Ramat Hahel (between Jerusalem and Bethlehem), and on the royal bench at the Ras Shamra palace in ivory relief. This tree is usually considered to be a symbol of the king's potency for channeling prosperity into the kingdom.[19] This particular depiction shows a goddess in the normal place of the tree. Since Asherah was herself symbolized by a post, a stylized tree, she is the most likely deity to be identified with this carving. Gray was quite convinced that this is an authentic Asherah depiction.[20] Moreover, he noted that the art is Mycenean, after the sytle of a seafaring people, who probably also knew her as a sea goddess, Lady Asherah of the Sea.[21]

C. The Qudshu Group

Negbi[22] has pointed out a certain group of six Qudshu plaques, so called because of an inscription on a stele describing the goddess as Qudshu-Ashtart-Anat. Qudshu was another name for Asherah, as shown in Chapter 1. In Egypt the identities of these three goddesses were obviously confused, perhaps merged together. All six of the female deities on these plaques bear the same Hathor-Isis hairdress (hair dropping to the shoulders on each side of the head with a curl at each shoulder), and three of them are shown standing on the back of a lion, as has been noted is often associated with Asherah. According to Schaeffer these plaques are, with a great degree of certainty, identifiable with Asherah.[23] Furthermore, one might also note that in these images she is often holding onto plants or animals, as was found on the ivory unguent box lid of Minet el-Beida. Four of these were actually found in Minet el-Beida, dated c1400-1200, one found at Acre, dated c1300, and the other at Zincirli, dated c1200-1100.[24] Also in this group, as Negbi[25] pointed out, are two other Qudshu goddesses found paired with divine mates. These couples consist of a smiting god (El) and his consort, who is known in the ancient texts to be none other than Asherah, Qudshu. Both of these couples, according to Negbi, can be dated c1300-1100, one found at Tel Nebi-Mend, the other at Minet el-Beida.[26]

D. Megiddo

Megiddo was an active Canaanite cult site from at least 2000 to 1200. It has been excavated by B. Schumacher, C. S. Fischer, P. L. O. Guy, and G. Loud before 1940, and by Y. Yadin and others since then. Its 20 levels extend from the pre-patriarchal Calcolithic Age to the 4th century B.C.E. Three Canaanite sanctuaries have been uncovered there, each with its own pedestal, suggesting that Megiddo supported and worshiped a triad of deities. Both the Canaanite myths and the artifacts discovered there suggest that the triad was El, Baal, and Asherah. Typically present at such places was an altar, a pillar (pedestal) representing El or Baal, and a wooden Asherah in the form of a post.

Negbi[27] has identified twelve female figurines from the Megiddo site as belonging to the same kind. They were all crudely molded, endowed with conical headgear, and at least four of them had their hands on either their breasts or their abdomens, suggesting that they were mother goddesses. Negbi dated all of them $_{c}$1800-1400. Since Asherah is the mother goddess, it is a strong possibility that they were intended to be Asherah images. And since they are in most ways similar to each other, all twelve of them could be Asherah images. Moreover, the description by May[28] of a terra-cotta figurine, found in a Megiddo tomb dated $_{c}$2000-1200, is a breast-holding mother goddess with a cylindrical headdress. This, for the same reasons stated about the metal figurines, that is, that they have the mother-goddess characteristics, is in all likelihood an Asherah image.

E. Nahariyah

On the coast, just south of Tyre at the mouth of the River Ga'aton, lies Nahariyah. Excavations in 1954-1955 uncovered three temple layers, as described by Dothan.[29] The bottom layer is an early temple and typical Canaanite high place. The middle layer is a late temple, a larger high place, and a pillar. The upper layer is a late temple and a smaller high place with a rectangular block on top of it. Some of the artifacts uncovered there are offering vessels, 7-wick saucer lamps, 7-cup bowls, bones of domestic animals in ashes, incense stands, beads of precious stones, semi-precious and precious metal jewelry, female deity figurines of bronze and silver, a stone mold for casting these figurines, and animal figurines. Dothan noted that it can be deduced from the nature and location of these artifacts that the cult practices included oil offerings poured on the high place, gift offerings placed there and in the other areas of the temple, and sacrificial feasts.

The design of the temples and high place at Nahariya is quite similar to that of Megiddo. The 7-cup bowls have also been discovered at Megiddo as well as the cult sites in Ras Shamra. Dothan argued that one might suppose then that the cultic practices in all of these places bore some similarity.

The female deity of Nahariya, based on its seacoast location near Tyre and Sidon, where Asherah was the local deity, was most likely Asherah, Lady Asherah of the Sea. Being itself a port location,

Nahariya was probably a place of worship not only for local inhabitants but also for shipping personnel who very likely carried their loyalty for Asherah both to Nahariya and from Nahariya. The date of the site, that is the active period of the cult, is c1800-1600.

Negbi[30] has described figurines discovered at the Nahariya site as the "Nahariya group." There are eight figurines and one casting mold. These are the figurines discovered at the Nahariya site. They all have the conical headgear as was found on the figurines of Megiddo, and their hands are either on their abdomens—the mold is of this type—or holding their breasts. These figurines, all found in the sacred area, suggest the mother goddess, Asherah.

F. Egypt

Five limestone depictions have been found in Egypt which are helpful in the process of identifying other artifacts in this study.[31] One is a nude goddess of the New Kingdom period, 1550-1090. It has the Hathor hairdress and depicts the goddess holding a serpent in one hand and a lotus in the other. She is standing on the back of a lion. A second nude goddess from the Nineteenth Dynasty, 1350-1200, also has the Hathor hairdress, is holding a serpent in each hand, is standing on the back of a lion, and is enscribed in hieroglyphics with the words, "Qadesh, the beloved of Ptah." Qadesh can easily be supposed to parallel Qudshu, and therefore suggests Asherah. A third depiction, not dated, shows the nude goddess holding a serpent in one hand and a lotus in the other, standing on the back of a lion. A fourth, found on a Nineteenth Dynasty stele, has the Hathor hairdress, is holding a lotus in one hand and a serpent in the other, and is standing on the back of a lion. An inscription underneath the goddess is particularly revealing. She is called Qadesh and stands between two male deities labelled Min and Resheph. Another part of the inscription is at the bottom of the panel directly below this one. The lower panel depicts a skirted, seated goddess, substantially different in appearance from the upper goddess. The inscription labels the lower goddess as Anat. Hence there is, at this time and place, a definite artistic distinction between Anat and the upper goddess,

Asherah. A fifth depiction is a New Kingdom nude goddess, in Hathor hairdress, holding a lotus in one hand and a serpent in the other, and standing on the back of a lion. Beneath it is an inscription calling her Qadesh.

The similar characteristics of these limestone depictions, when considered along with the inscriptions labelling them as Qadesh, the Holy One known to be Asherah, and when considered as compared to the characteristics of goddess figurines found in Palestine in the same period, give weight to the argument that these and similar depictions are of the Canaanite goddess, Asherah.

One might ask what these Canaanite goddess depictions are doing in Egypt. The fact of frequent commerce between Egypt and the coastal cities of Palestine is sufficient explanation.

G. Lachish

A Canaanite temple has been excavated at Lachish, one of the largest of Judah's southern cities, dating from $_{c}$1500. Its most recent and most extensive excavation was conducted by D. Ussishkin.[32] At this temple site was found a terracotta ewer, bearing the inscription of a goddess named Elath. Elath is, of course, Asherah in the Baal myths. Kenyon[33] has observed that since inscriptions, such as this one, found on ewers are usually dedicatory in nature, dedicating the ewer and its contents to the deity named in the inscription, one can assume that Asherah worship was taking place at the temple site in Lachish in such a form that offerings were being brought to her. Negbi strengthened the argument for the presence of an Asherah cult there, noting the discovery of a Late Bronze Age divine couple figurine set, being the smiting god, El, and his consort, Asherah.[34]

H. Ekron

One of the five Philistine cities, biblical Ekron, lies west of Jerusalem where the coastal plain joins the Shephelah. The modern site is called Tel Miqne, on the property of Kibbutz Revadim. In the seventh season of its excavation, in 1987, under the direction of Trude Dothan and Sy Gitin, and with the assistance of this author, an Asherah plaque was discovered and identified. The terra cotta plaque was in fair condition, however only the upper half of the plaque was found. Clay had been pressed onto a mold to form the image of Asherah, visible from the waist up. The face was chipped off. Her hair was in the shape of the Hathor headdress and her arms were raised, holding what appeared to be a snake in each hand. The plaque, about 7 cm. square, was found in a pre-Philistine strata near the acropolis of the city, dated approximately 13th century Canaanite.[35]

I. Bethel

A cylinder seal was discovered at Bethel, dated $_{c}$1300, which depicts two deities. One is a war god and the other is named by a hieroglyphic inscription as Astart. The war god of the Baal myths is Baal himself, but the goddess associated with him is usually his wife, Anat. The Hebrew Scriptures cast a greater shadow over the identity of this goddess in that Ashtoreth (Astarte) is the consort of Baal in Jg 2:13 and 10:6, and I Sam 7:4 and 12:10, but in I Kg 18:19 the partner of Baal is called Asherah by Jezebel who came from Tyre, a known Asherah worship center. Because of the fluidity of the names, the identification of this goddess as Asherah cannot be certain. Neither can it be ruled out. The conical hat she wears may add slightly to the argument that she is Asherah.[36]

J. Taanach

At Taanach, around 900 B.C.E., there was in use a libation stand in the area of the Canaanite sanctuary. It has four panels, one above the other, with carvings on each panel. The bottom panel is a nude goddess with Hathor hairdress, hands held up, and flanked by two lions. The second panel is two winged sphinxes, each bearing the Hathor hairdress. The third panel is a stylized tree of life with two goats eating from it. Next to each goat is a lion, both of which are almost identical to the lions on the bottom panel. The top panel is a bull and a sun.

The bottom and the third panel are a parallelism in clay. On the bottom is an Asherah image and on the third is the stylized tree of life, both of which are flanked by lions. One recalls the unguent box lid of Minet el-Beida on which the goddess was substituted for the usual tree of life. This parallelism supports identification of the Minet el-Beida piece as an Asherah image. The second panel, with sphinxes in Asherah's usual hairdress, is a poetic parody of the bottom and third panels. The bull is the usual symbol for El in the Canaanite pantheon. As chief of the pantheon, El's image belongs at the top of the libation stand and joined with his divine consort, Asherah. Lapp has identified the goddess on the stand as Astarte. He is obviously mistaken. Dever argued that the goddess is Asherah, and defended the general premise of associating Asherah with lions, considering not only the numerous depictions already cited in this study, but also an inscription written on a $_{c}$1200 arrowhead found at el-Khader, designating it in Canaanite as the property of someone called Servant of the Lion Lady.[37]

K. Jerusalem

In a garden in Jerusalem's Ecole Biblique, there is a Hebrew burial place, dated $_{c}$800-700, consisting of bench tombs with carvings on the headrests. On several of the headrests is the Hathor hairdress[38], so commonly associated with Asherah, thereby suggesting that Asherah is associated with the funerary cult of the Israelites in Judah. This artifact is especially significant, according to Dever, because "funerary practices are among the most conservative and yet the most revealing expressions of folk religion in primitive societies."[39]

L. Elephantine

In Egypt on an island in the south segment of the Nile, just north of the Aswan dam, there have been discovered the remnants of a diaspora community, an Aramaic-speaking Jewish military colony from $_{c}$600, called Elephantine. It contained a temple of Yaho, presumably Yahweh. The Egyptian city nearest Elephantine contained a temple to the "queen of heaven." In trying to identify this queen of heaven, Porten[40] suggested that it is Anat, because of the double appearance of her name in the Elephantine texts. However, he admitted the weakness in his argument, saying that in the Hebrew Scriptures there appears not even one condemnation of the worship of Anat, but frequent condemnations of Asherah worship, and also of Astarte worship. He also noted that it was the women of Egypt who seemed to be the primary instigators of worship of the queen of heaven, just as they were recorded in the Hebrew Scriptures as instigatiors of Asherah worship in Israel (I Kg 15:13, 16:33, 18:19; II Chr 15:16). He noted further that in Ex 34:13f there is an expressed prohibition of marriage with foreign peoples for fear that it would lead to idolatry. Given the evidence against his suggestion, Porten's idea that the queen of heaven was Anat could easily be changed to suggest that it was Asherah, or even Astarte, although Asherah seems the more likely of the two. Moreover, given the existence of the Egyptian stele confusing Qudshu with Astarte and Anat[41], the possibility of naming the queen of heaven as Anat is even less certain.

M. Sidon

Maurice Dunand has excavated a large temple area near Sidon.[42] It is a sixth century Neo-Babylonian style complex. In the Temple area, there is a room with a throne and a pool, which he described, in the absence of any inscriptions to indicate such, as the chapel of the throne of Astarte. J. W. Betlyon has re-examined the data, and now believes that this chapel should be attributed not to Astarte, but to Asherah/Elat, the goddess of Sidon.[43] His argument is based on the marine background of Asherah–hence, the pool–and other evidence of an active Asherah cult at Sidon during the sixth and fifth centuries.

The figurines and other artifacts described in this chapter will endorse the claim that Asherah worship was active in Judah and Israel during the Middle and Late Bronze Ages, i.e., during the time of the monarchy. While no individual artifact can completely verify this claim, nevertheless the accumulation of items leaves the impression that they are sufficient to corroborate it.

The mother-goddess figurines and other artifacts described in this chapter are an intriguing collection. It is in many instances difficult to identify them. The occasional inscription, e.g., the words on the Egyptian plaque mentioned in Sub-section C, help to build the argument that certain characteristics are common on Asherah representations. These characteristics are at least the Hathor-Isis hairdress, the lion, hands holding the abdomen or breasts, and perhaps the serpent. As a group, these artifacts suggest that there was Asherah worship in the Canaanite territories during the time of the monarchy. This supports the evidence found in the Hebrew Bible, which suggests the same.

Notes

1 Kathleen Kenyon, *Amorites and Canaanites* (London: Oxford University Press, 1966), pp. 52-76; William Foxwell Albright, *Yahweh and the Gods of Canaan: A Historical Analysis of Two Contrasting Faiths* (London: Athlone Press, 1968); John Bright, *A History of Israel*, 3rd ed. (Philadelphia: Westminster Press, 1981); Martin Noth, *The History of Israel*, 2nd ed. (New York: Harper & Row, 1960); and John Gray, *The Canaanites*, Ancient Peoples and Places, no. 38 (London: Thames and Hudson, 1964).

2 Kathleen Kenyon, *Archaeology in the Holy Land*, 3rd ed. (London: Ernest Benn, 1970), pp. 162-63, 202-9.

3 William Foxwell Albright, "The Isrealite Conquest of Canaan in the Light of Archaeology," *Bulletin of the American Schools of Oriental Research* 74 (1939): 11-39.

4 Albrecht Alt, "The Settlement of the Israelites in Palestine," *Essays on Old Testament History and Religion* (Garden City, New York: Doubleday, 1978), pp. 173-221; Martin Noth, *History*.

5 George Mendenhall, "The Hebrew Conquest of Palestine," *Biblical Archaeology* 25 (1962): 66-87; Phillip J. King, "The Contribution of Archaeology to Biblical Studies," *Catholic Biblical Quarterly* 45 (January 1983): 4-7; and Norman K. Gottwald, *The Tribes of Yahweh* (Maryknoll, New York: Orbis Books, 1979).

6 For more on these matters, see Gottwald, *The Tribes of Yahweh*.

7 Ora Negbi, *Canaanite Gods in Metal: An Archaeological Study of Ancient Syro-Palestinian Figurines* (Tel Aviv: Tel Aviv University Institute of Archaeology, 1976), pp. 75, 83, 89, 102-3.

8 James Robert Engle, *Pillar Figurines of Iron Age Israel and Asherah/Asherim*, a dissertation for the University of Pittsburgh (Ann Arbor: University Microfilms International, 1980).

9 For example, Thomas A. Holland, "A Study of Palestinian Iron Age Baked Clay Figurines," *Levant* 9 (1977): 124.

10 Engle, *Pillar Figurines*, pp. 34-35.

11 John Gray, *The Canaanites*, Ancient Peoples and Places, no. 38 (London: Thames and Hudson, 1964), p. 66.

12 Negbi, *Gods in Metal*, p. 141.

13 Kathleen Kenyon, *Amorites and Canaanites* (London: Oxford University Press, 1966), p. 58.

14 Negbi, *Gods in Metal*, p. 108; A. G. Barrois, *Manuel d'archaeologie Biblique* (Paris: A. and J. Picard, 1953), p. 396; James B. Pritchard, *The Ancient Near East in Pictures Relating to the Old Testament*, 2nd ed. with supp. (New Jersey: Princeton University Press, 1969), pl. 465, 522-26.

15 Pritchard, *The ANE in Pictures*, pl. 829.

16 John Gray, *The KRT Text in the Literature of Ras Shamra*, 2nd ed. (Leiden: E. J. Brill, 1964), p. 59.

17 C. F. A. Schaeffer, *Syria* 31 (1954): pl. 8.

18 Gray, *Canaanites*, pl. 32; Pritchard, *The ANE in Pictures*, pl. 464; A. G. Barrois, *Manuel d'archeologie*, pp. 394-395.

19 John Gray, *Near Eastern Mythology* (New York: Hamlyn Publishing Group, 1969), p. 62.

20 John Gray, "Ugarit," in *Archaeology and Old Testament Study*, ed. D. Winton Thomas (Oxford: Clarendon Press, 1967), pp. 145-67.

21 See also Cyrus H. Gordon, *Ugarit and Minoan Crete: The Bearing of Their Texts on the Origins of Western Culture* (New York: W. W. Norton, 1966).

22 Negbi, *Gods in Metal*, pp. 99-100, 113, 115-17; Pritchard, *The ANE in Pictures*, pl. 830.

23 C. F. A. Schaeffer, "Le fouilles de Minet-el-Beida et de Ras Shamra," *Syria* 13 (1932): pl. 9; John Gray, *Canaanites*, pl. 29.

24 Frank Moore Cross, *Canaanite Myth and Hebrew Epic* (Cambridge: Harvard University Press, 1973), pp. 19, 33-34; Pritchard, *The ANE in Pictures*, pl. 830.

25 Negbi, *Gods in Metal*, pp. 99-100, 113, 115-17.

26 In a thoroughly written analysis, Christa Clamer has described a Late Bronze Age gold plaque from the Lachish temple area. ("A Gold Plaque from Tel Lachish," *Tel Aviv* 7 (1980): 152-162.) The plaque depicts a Qudshu goddess whom she hesitantly identified as Astarte. Since she admits that there is no proof for this identification, and since some of the characteristics of the goddess are similar to Asherah depictions, there may be room to suggest that this is an Asherah plaque.

Another depiction, a pottery mould from Tel Qarnayim in the Beth-Shean valley (not dated[!] but probably Late Bronze Age), was described by Sara Ben-Arieh as a nude goddess with Hathor characteristics and a conical hat. ("A Mould for a Goddess Plaque," *Israel Exploration Journal* 33 (1983): 72-77. See also "A Pottery Mould for a Goddess Figurine," *Kadmoniat* 16 (1983): 123-124. [Hebrew]) Ben-Arieh suggested that the deity is in the Qudshu group, but does not choose from the two most likely candidates, Astarte and Asherah.

27 Negbi, *Gods in Metal*, pp. 64-66; Gray, *Canaanites*, p. 70; G. Ernest Wright, *Biblical Archaeology*, 2nd ed. (Philadelphia: Westminster Press, 1962), pp. 114, 116-17.

28 H. G. May, "Material Remains of the Megiddo Cult," *Oriental Institute Publications* 26 (1935): 27-30; Pritchard, *The ANE in Pictures*, pl. 467.

29 M. Dothan, "The Excavations at Nahariyah," *Israel Exploration Journal* 6 (1956): 14-25; Yohanan Aharoni, *The Archaeology of the Land of Israel from the Prehistoric Beginnings to the End of the First Temple Period*, ed. Miriam Aharoni, trans. Anson F. Rainey (Philadelphia: Westminster Press, 1982), pl. 22A.

30 Negbi, *Gods in Metal*, p. 64.

31 Pritchard, *The ANE in Pictures*, pl. 470-74; Gray, *Canaanites*, pl. 20.

32 D. Ussishkin, "Excavations at Tel Lachish: 1973-1977, A Preliminary Report," *Tel Aviv* 5 (1978): 1-97.

33 Kathleen M. Kenyon, *The Bible and Recent Archaeology* (Atlanta: John Knox, 1978), p. 27.

34 Negbi, *Gods in Metal*, p. 141.

35 With the permission of the excavators of the Tel Miqne-Ekron Excavation Project, Trude Dothan and Seymour Gitin.

36 Pritchard, *The ANE in Pictures*, pl. 468.

37 Paul W. Lapp, "The 1968 Excavations at Tell Ta annek," *Bulletin of the American Schools of Oriental Research* 195 (1969): 42-49; William G. Dever, "Recent Archaeological Confirmation of the Cult of Asherah in Ancient Israel," *Hebrew Studies* 23 (1982): 40; King, "Contributions," p. 14.

38 See above, Section 3, Sub-section C.

39 Dever, "Recent Archaeological Confirmation," pp. 37-43; G. Barkay, A. Mazar, and A. Kloner, "The Northern Cemetery of Jerusalem in First Temple Times," *Qadmoniot* 8 (1975): 2-4.

40 Bezalel Porten, *Archives from Elephantine: The Life of an Ancient Jewish Military Colony* (Berkeley: University of California Press, 1968), pp. 176-79.

41 See above, Section 3, Sub-section C.

42 Maurice Dunand, "Le Temple d'Echmoun a Sidon: Essai de chronologie," *Bulletin du muses de Beyrouth* 26 (1973): 10-12.

43 John Wilson Betlyon, "The Cult of Asherah/Elat at Sidon," *Journal of Near Eastern Studies* 44(1985): 53-56.

Chapter 10

Inscriptions

Archaeologists are usually pleased to find tablets or carvings which include words. The written word can provide information not always available from other artifacts. It is fortunate that there are five such inscriptions which mention the goddess, Asherah. They show that there were oracles, wizardry, and fortune-telling associated with the cult of Asherah. They also support the contention that Asherah was worshiped by the Israelites and was considered to be the divine consort of Yahweh.

1. Inscriptions

The following is a list of Asherah-related inscriptions made available through archaeological discovery.

A. Taanach

Taanach, now Tel Taaneck, is six miles SSE of Megiddo. This large tel is the site of the ancient city of Taanach, founded 2700 and existing as a city through 1000. It was excavated in 1902-4 and again in 1963-68. Among the excavations there is a Middle Bronze Age (1800-1500) fortified area, where a tablet was discovered containing the Canaanite phrase "If the finger of Ashirat points [...]."[1] This implies that there were oracles of Asherah at this site.

B. Taanach

Albright[2] has translated several letters found inscribed on clay at Taanach. They can be dated $_c$1450. The beginning of one of them is quoted here:

> To Rewassa say, thus Guli-Adad. Live well! May the gods take note of thy welfare, the welfare of thy house, of thy children! Thou hast written to me with regard to silver, and behold I will give 50 shekels of silver—verily I will do [so]! Further, why dost thou not send thy greeting to me? And everything that thou hearest from there write to me. Further, and if there is a wizard of Asherah (*u-ma-an A-ši-rat*), let him tell our fortunes, and let me hear quickly (?); and the [oracular] sign and interpretation send to me. With regard to thy daughter...

This letter, written by Guli-Adad to his prince, contains evidence that at Taanach there was a wizard of Asherah at times available for oracles. The implication is that the Asherah cult is developed at this time to a rather advanced state in which wizardry is practiced by the power of Asherah, and is anxiously sought by patrons seeking the telling of fortunes.

C. Kuntillet Ajrud

Recent years have given rise to some attentive debate in the scholarly community regarding inscriptions found on jars at Kuntillet Ajrud. This Sinai excavation was directed by Ze'ev Meshel of Tel Aviv University in 1975-76 at Kuntillet Ajrud, which is 40 miles south of Kadesh Barnea and 55 miles northwest of Eilat, almost at the Negev border. Its principle building appears to be a stopping place for passing traders and a guard station to protect this crossroads site. Found there were many plastered walls and large storage jars, pithoi, on which there are crudely painted inscriptions and drawings. They are in paleo-Hebrew and are dated on paleographic grounds to the first half of the eighth century.[3] One of them reads:

> brktk lyhwh tmn wlʾšrth[4]
> I bless you by Yahweh of Teiman and by his Asherah.

Another reads:

> brkt ʾtkm ljhwh šmrn wlʾšrth[5]
> I have blessed you by Yahweh *šmrn* and his Asherah.

Emerton[6] has concluded that Yahweh *šmrn* is Yahweh of Samaria, written by a traveler from Samaria passing through this way-station for southern journeys. He cited parallels from Canaanite literature which, coming from the territories nearer Samaria than Kuntillet Ajrud, demonstrate the common usage of the name of a deity in association with a place, usually a place of worship. These citations include Anat of Saphon (*ʿnt ṣpn*) from RS 24.253.13-14, Asherah of the Tyrians (*ʾaṯrt ṣrm*) from CTA 14.4.201, and Elath of the Sydonians (*ʾilt sdynm*) from CTA 14.4.202. Meshel, on the other hand, originally posited the *šmrn* as the active qal participle of the verb *šamar*, translating it "who guards us." Meshel later followed Gilula in agreeing that it means Samaria, as was reported by Weinfeld.[7]

In this inscription the question arises, in the absence of internal evidence, whether the Asherah is the proper name of a goddess or a common noun indicating a more general reference to female goddesses. Gilula, in the same work cited above, stated that it could be either of these, but that in either case one can infer that Asherah is the consort of Yahweh. Meshel conceded that Asherah could be construed here as Yahweh's consort, but it remains a mere unproven possibility. He suggested three possibilities for interpreting the Asherah. First, it could be a reference to a generic female deity, but he added that there is no evidence to substantiate this possibility. Second, it could be a reference to the cult object which, in the Hebrew scriptures, is used to represent the goddess Asherah. Third, as suggested by Lipinski,[8] it could be a reference to a sacred place, a shrine called Asherah. This third suggestion, he points out, is difficult to reconcile with the Hebrew Scriptures. Since only the second suggestion reconciles with the Hebrew Scriptures, Meshel chose it as the most likely possibility, thereby presuming that Asherah is a common noun in the inscription.

In contrast to Meshel, Emerton said that there is no difficulty in supposing that Asherah is a consort of Yahweh.[9] The cult was syncretistic. But he said there is no proof either. The difficulty is in the grammatical structure. There is no Hebrew precedent for the suffix of possession used with a personal name. One should not suppose that such is the case unless no suitable alternative is found. So he ended by agreeing with Meshel that as long as Meshel's second suggestion remains viable, one may not assume that Asherah is here intended to be a goddess.

Freedman was quite clear in saying that this construction, though grammatically unusual, should not be discounted as impossible. He is convinced that it speaks not of a cult object, but of the goddess herself, and should be translated as "his Asherah," with a capital A.[10]

These blessing formulas show that God had an Asherah, noted Lemaire[11], but do not describe what his Asherah was—deity, cult object, or anything at all. He supposed[12] that Asherah is a generic name for a live tree or a small group of trees, but did not offer arguments against the "post" indications in the biblical texts. He also did not account for the biblical texts in which Asherah is clearly not a post or a tree, but a deity, as in I Kgs 15:13. He did say, however, that

> it is on the way to being personified, as reflected in the way the asherah is associated with Yahweh in blessing. In a more subtle psychological or theological way, we are witnessing a kind of birth of a hypostasis in which the essence of the divine is bound to a cultic object; that is, an aspect of the divine is becoming concretized or reified—and may soon rival God himself.[13]

To this one might reply that the deuteronomistic writers, who must certainly have been aware of this trend, reflected this fear in their writing. But given the existence of a deity by that name in Canaanite culture, one might more readily suppose that they feared a deity and her cult, who rivalled or partnered with Yahweh, rather than a tree.

Dever[14] disagreed with Emerton. He said that the suffix does not rule out a personal interpretation of Asherah. His argument is based on a drawing found directly under the inscription on the jar, where there is a goddess seated near two lions, and next to that a tree of life with two goats eating from it. Meshel had thought the drawing was of the goddess Bes, and Gilula ignored it entirely. Dever saw it as sufficiently characteristic of other Asherah depictions to claim that he is quite certain that it is Asherah. He thus added weight to his claim that the inscription refers not merely to a cult object, but to the goddess.

Lemaire[15] disagreed with the interpretation of this figure as Bes or as Asherah. He claimed that there is not enough detail on it to associate it with anyone in particular. He suggested that it not be used to shed light on the inscription. Parhiya Beck claimed that both of the standing figures are Bes, but not the seated one.[16]

A second jar is inscribed with the following:

jhwh tmn wʾšrth
Yahweh Teman and his Asherah.

Teman in this case, as shown by Dever[17], refers to the region of Edom. Pictured along with the inscription is not only a cow suckling her calf, but also two lions. Arguments similar to those suggested for the first inscription will lead one to conclude that this text and its accompanying drawings may refer to the goddess Asherah. One cannot conclude, however, considering these inscriptions, that Asherah was thereby viewed as the consort of Yahweh. The precise nature of the association of Yahweh and Asherah in these inscriptions is not clear.[18]

D. Arslan Tash

Arslan Tash is in northern Syria, about 120 miles northeast of Ras Shamra and 22 miles east of Carchemish. It was an Assyrian city called Hadatu and a provincial center. There was a temple of Ishtar on the site. A household plaque was found there dating from $_c$700, written in a Phoenician dialect quite similar to biblical Hebrew. It was addressed as a warning to malevolent deities. The relevant part of the text is translated by Cross and Saley.[19]

5) bat ʾbʾ
6) bl tbʾn
7) wḥṣr ʾdrk
8) bl tdrkn k(r)
9) rt ln ʾlt
10) ʿlm ʾšr krt

11) ln wkl bn ʾlm
12) wrb dr kl qdšn

5) The house I enter
6) ye shall not enter;
7) And the court I tread,
8) ye shall not tread,
9) The Eternal One has made a covenant with us,
10) Asherah has made (a pact)
11) with us, And all the sons of El,
12) and the great of the council of all the Holy Ones.

This text gives witness to two points. First, there was Asherah worship in northern Syria, quite far inland, around 700. Second, she was a household deity, showing that she was worshiped by the people of the area.

E. Khirbet el-Qom

In 1967 William B. Dever, at the Hebrew Union College, acquired about 125 eighth century artifacts on the Jerusalem antiquities market. After some intrigue he traced them to Khirbet el-Qom, a small Arab village 8 miles west of Hebron. There he found their source, a group of Hebrew tombs. He began a salvage excavation immediately. He dated all the inscriptions to the eighth century by the shape, stance, and form of the characters. Identified with Saphir found in Micah 1:11, it is a funerary inscription carved into the cave wall above a tomb. Inscription no. 3, the only one relevant to this study, was difficult to read for two reasons. First, it was created by scratching onto the soft rock of the tomb. Second, most of line three was scratched twice, and the engraver was not always careful enough to scratch exactly on the same lines, so that some of the letters are doubled, producing a somewhat confusing effect.[20] As it was published by Lemaire, the text reads:[21]

1) ʾryhw.hʿšr.ktbh
2) brk.ʾryhw.lyhwh

3) whṣryh.l ʾsrth.hwš ʿlh
4) lʾnywh

Lemaire translated it as follows:

1) Uriyahu, the Rich, had this written:
2) May Uriyahu be blessed by Yahweh
3) And from his enemies may he be saved by his Asherah.
4) by Onyahu

The first to publish this text was Dever.[22] He supposed that the word Asherah in line three should be translated as "the hand of whoever." He based this on what appeared to be a correction of the original, a "d" transcribed over the original "h," changing what would have been Asherah into the word for hand. This superscription, however, is not necessarily the work of the original scribe, a fact which Dever did not account for and cannot be presumed. Lemaire's later translation of this word as Asherah seems, therefore, the more likely. One notes further that this is almost exactly parallel with the inscription found at Kuntillet Ajrud. Both forms use the unusual feminine construct. Both, then, could be considered identical in their relevance to the goddess, Asherah.

Lemaire originally identified this Asherah as a wooden pole, the cult object suggested in Dt 16:21-22. In other words, he considered it to be the sacred tree, but not the goddess herself. Dever,[23] in a later consideration, recognized the likelihood of the translation of Asherah over and above that of hand, and himself suggested that it must be the goddess and not merely the cult object. He based his argument on the mounting evidence that Asherah was worshiped in Judah at this time and on the fact that this formula is in the form of a blessing, demanding the attention of the goddess herself more than that of her cultic representation.[24]

In a later revised version, Lemaire added a translation for two other fragments, lines 5 and 6.[25] The complete revised translation reads:

1) Uryahu the wealthy man had it written:
2) Blessed be Uryahu by Yahweh

3) and by his asherah; from his enemies he saved him!
4) [written] by Onyahu
5) ...and by his asherah
6) ...[and by] his [ashe]r[ah]

Lines 5 and 6 were not identified by Dever as part of the inscription. Lemaire recognized line 5 as *lʾšrh*. Line 6 is a partial copy of line 5, damaged at the edge of the stone fragment. His argument for changing the translation's word order in line 5 is the following:

> I have changed the position of "by his asherah" in line 3; in the original it appears after "enemies." I believe that the engraver, working in the dark of the tomb with only an oil lamp for light, made a mistake, perhaps forgetting to carve "by his asherah" at the beginning of the line and then writing it after "from his enemies."[26]

He is certain now that the inscription does indeed read "Asherah," and describes it as a blessing formula that was probably common in the eighth century.

The Khirbet el-Qom inscription, therefore, testifies to the following: As an element of a funerary inscription, Asherah worship must have been a part of popular Hebrew piety in the area of Judah in 800-700 B.C.E. As associated with Yahweh, it is evident that this popular piety was not purist.

It is evident that none of the archaeological discoveries taken alone proves very much about Asherah worship in Palestine. Some of the artifacts are identifiable with Asherah with certainty, while many are uncertain. Considered as a group, however, they contain certain implications. The common characteristics of these images, coupled with a few rather helpful inscriptions, leave the impression that there was Asherah worship in the Middle and Late Bronze Ages in Canaanite territories. In the Iron Age, when the Israelites began their life in the Canaanite hill country, Asherah images began to turn up in their lands and even in their inscriptions. Asherah was worshiped in Palestine both by the Canaanites and the Israelites.

Notes

1 Jack Finegan, *Light from the Ancient Past: The Archaeological Background of Judaism and Christianity*, 2nd ed. (New Jersey: Princeton University Press, 1959), p. 168.

2 William Foxwell Albright, "A Prince of Taanach in the Fifteenth Century B.C.," *Bulletin of the American Schools of Oriental Research* 94 (1944): 12-27.

3 Andre Lemaire, "Who or What Was Yahweh's Asherah," *Biblical Archaeology Review* 10 (1984): 44.

4 Pithos 2, lines 4-6.

5 Pithos 1, lines 1-2.

6 J. A. Emerton, "New Light on Israelite Religion: The Implications of the Inscriptions from Kuntillet Ajrud," *Zeitschrift für die alttestamentliche Wissenschaft* 94 (1982): 2-20.

7 Z. Meshel, "Did Yahweh Have a Consort?" The New Religious Inscriptions from the Sinai," *Biblical Archaeological Review* 5 (1979): 24-35; Mordecai Gilula, "To Yahweh Shomron and His Asherah," (Hebrew) *Schnaton* 3 (1978-1979): 129-137; M. Weinfeld, "A Discussion of S. Meshel's Two Publications of 1978-1979," (Hebrew) *Schnaton* 4 (1980): 280-84.

8 Edward Lipinski, "The Goddess Atirat in Ancient Arabia, in Babylon, and in Ugarit," *Orientalia Lovaniensia Periodica* 3 (1972): 101-119.

9 Emerton, "New Light," pp.2-20.

10 David Noel Freedman, "Yahweh of Samaria and His Asherah," *Biblical Archaeologist* (December, 1987): 241-249.

11 Lemaire, "Who and What," pp. 42-51.

12 Lemaire, "Who and What," pp. 50-51.

13 Lemaire, "Who and What," p. 51.

14 William G. Dever, "Recent Archaeological Confirmation of the Cult of Asherah in Ancient Israel," *Hebrew Studies* 23 (1982): 37-43.

15 Lemaire, "Who and What," pp. 45-6.

16 Parhiya Beck, "The Drawings from Horvat Teiman (Kuntillet Ajrud)," *Tel Aviv* 9 (1982): 29-31.

17 Dever, "Archaeological Confirmation," pp. 37-43.

18 Philip J. King, "The Contribution of Archaeology to Biblical Studies," *Catholic Biblical Quarterly* 45 (1983): 1-16.

19 Text and translation from F. M. Cross and R. J. Saley, "Phoenecian Incantations on a Plaque of the Seventh Century B.C. from Arslan Tash in Upper Syria," *Bulletin of the American Schools of Oriental Research* 197 (1970): 48-49; some discussion is in James Robert Engle, *Pillar Figurines of Iron Age Israel and Asherah/Asherim*, a dissertation for the University of Pittsburgh (Ann Arbor: University Microfilms International, 1980), pp. 85-87.

20 Lemaire, "Who and What," pp. 42-43.

21 Andre Lemaire, "Les Inscriptions de Khirbet El Qom et Le' Asherah de YHWH," *Revue Biblique* 4 (1977): 595-608.

22 William G. Dever, "Iron Age Epigraphic Material from Khirbet El-Kom," *Hebrew Union College Annual* 50-51 (1969-1970): 139-204.

23 Dever, "Archaeological Confirmation," pp. 37-43.

24 See also Engle, *Pillar Figurines*, pp. 81-83; King, "Contribution of Archaeology," p. 14; Emerton, "New Light," p. 6.

25 Lemaire, "Who or What," p. 44, and p. 43 for a very clear photo and drawing.

26 Lemaire, "Who or What," p. 44.

PART IV

CULMINATION

After studying her ancient backgrounds, her biblical references, and her artifacts, what can one understand about Asherah?

Chapter 11

Asherah: Goddess of Israel?

The goddess described in the Ugaritic texts was originally a sea goddess. This was undoubtedly in complementarity with Baal, who was in charge of fertility. She was the consort of El, the chief god of the Canaanite pantheon, and as such held the highest rank among the female deities of Canaan. Being the consort of El inevitably led to Asherah's receiving the title "progenetrix of the gods." It was because of this title that Asherah was viewed as a nurturing goddess.

Her role as mother-goddess dominates Ugarit's understanding of her divine character, as is reflected in the Keret epic in which Yasab, the offspring of the King of Ugarit, is suckled by Asherah. This is a clear indication that the Asherah was viewed as the mother of the kings of Ugarit. Futhermore, the Keret epic reveals that the people of Ugarit were engaged in an active cult of Asherah worship, including sanctuaries, cult officials, and offerings. The non-aquatic setting of this epic and other texts indicats that Asherah's sphere of influence moved beyond the sea to the inland territories, where the people of Israel lived.

The distinction between goddesses was not always clear. Even though they had separate names, they often were portrayed as having similar characteristics.

The fact that there were deities outside of Ugarit who shared similarities of name and/or characteristics with Asherah, e.g., Ishtar of Assyria and Ashratu of the Amorites, suggests that in the ancient near east the role of such a goddess and even the name tended to be transported from one ancient nation to another, from one pantheon to another. This is an important observation in a study which suggests that the Canaanite goddess, Asherah, was adopted by at least part of the Israelite community. In the Hebrew Bible there is confusion between Asherah and Astarte, even though Astarte is a lesser fertility goddess in Ugarit. They have not only similar characteristics, but similar names.

William L. Reed was the first in modern times to give serious attention to Asherah in the Hebrew Bible as a goddess. He concluded that when the word "Asherah" appears in the Hebrew Bible, it sometimes refers to the deity named Asherah, and sometimes to the wooden post used as a cult object in the service of the goddess Asherah. Reed claimed that, considering the biblical texts, Asherah was worshiped in Israel throughout the period of the monarchy.

The work of Reed, however, is perhaps unwittingly challenged by Yamashita. He noted that Asherah occurs either in deuteronomistic texts or in texts which are in some way dependent on the deuteronomistic history. This raises an important question about Reed's study. Is it possible that the deuteronomistic historian has inserted his own prejudice against Asherah worship into the texts? Is it then possible that Asherah worship was not necessarily known throughout the monarchy but only during the Josian reform, the focal point of the deuteronomist's concerns? Yamashita did not raise this question nor did he answer it.

There are arguments against this possibility. The first is embarrassment. It was embarrassing for the deuteronomist to have to admit that his people worshiped Asherah. If the deuteronomist had known of Asherah only in the decades of Josiah, it is unlikely that he would have extended the abuse so far back into his own history, thus compounding the embarrassment. Even granting that the deuteronomist was looking for explanations for Israel's punishment with exile, it is still not likely that he would have extended this abuse as far back as the early monarchy. Had it occurred only once, e.g., during the reign of Manasseh, that would have been sufficient to make his point.

A second and stronger argument has to do with the roots of the goddess, Asherah, in Canaan. Given the choice of suggesting either a continuing presence of Asherah worship during the time of Josiah after several centuries of the absence of such worship or an unexplained reappearance of Asherah worship during the time of Josiah after several centuries of the absence of such worship, the former suggestion seems the more likely. In order to suggest the reappearance of Asherah worship around the time of Josiah, one would have to account for it. There is no explanation of why there might have been a sudden resurgence of the worship of a pagan goddess long forgotten. The more likely proposition is that the worship of Asherah was never forgotten. Though it may have waxed and waned, its existence as late as the time of Josiah is best explained by saying that Asherah worship was never fully discontinued.

A third argument is that the Chronicler, although writing from a different theological standpoint from the deuteronomist, nevertheless retained the full range of Asherah texts. Since the Chronicler did not share the theological biases of the deuteronomist, one would expect him to be free of the Asherah texts if they were truly an exaggeration of the deuteronomist. But such is not the case. The Chronicler sustains all the deuteronomistic reports about Asherah.

The last argument is the literary argument. The stereotypical language of the deuteronomistic redactor(s) suggests that Asherah worship was deeply embedded in the religion of Israel throughout the monarchic period. By noting the pattern of the use of Asherah with altar, pillar, idol, and high place it becomes clear that the deuteronomist was using a meta-formula (this author's own term) in which the deuteronomist implied that the Asherah is an important cultic aberration associated with the altar, pillars, and idols at the high place. The Asherah was part of the foreign syncretism in the Hebrew cult, a cultic aberration. Further, it shows the central place which this particular aberration occupied in the deuteronomic reforms, an aberration which apparently had lasted the entire length of the monarchy. The worship of Asherah had held a central place in the pagan Canaanite cult. Its destruction was imperative if the deuteronomistic reform was to protect Israel's strict monotheism and keep it from henotheism.

From the passages in Deuteronomy there emerged the suggestion that the Asherah is a particular kind of idol, a wooden representation of Asherah. Fequently reinforced by other biblical texts, this notion is undoubtedly a source of confusion among those who posit that Asherah is a tree, even for the LXX translator who constantly translated Asherahs as groves of trees. Their mistake is to fail to realize that the wooden Asherah was an idol, a human-made object rather than a tree or grove standing unaltered by human hands.

An amazing development, found first in the text of Dt 16:21, is that the Asherah pole was erected in the Jerusalem Temple right next to the altar of Yahweh. This implies Asherah worship was so accepted by the people that she was worshiped right along with Yahweh in the Temple. This is the pinnacle of syncretism, the joining of religions at the very highest level, the official Temple cult. It is almost startling to realize that the Hebrews, who saw their living God present in the Temple, believed that a living Asherah was equally present at their worship, and that Yahweh and Asherah were probably viewed as a divine couple. Olyan declared, "It is important to note that we are not speaking only of popular religion here; the asherahs of Samaria, Bethel and Jerusalem were a consituent part of state Yahwism."[1]

The texts of Judges emphasize that Israel did not abandon Yahweh to go over and worship Asherah, but that they worshiped Yahweh and Asherah simultaneously, even as consorts. They were henotheistic. The texts also indicate that Asherah worship was by far the popular choice, and that reformers like Gideon were in the minority.

In spite of several noteworthy attempts to eliminate Asherah worship from the land, such reform was fervently resisted by popular piety. In the texts of Kings it is evident that the Asherah was considered both a deity and a cult object which represented her. Worship of Asherah was not viewed, in the eyes of popular piety, as in conflict with Yahwism. It was seen, rather, as harmonious with the worship of Yahweh. This was not, of course, the view of deuteronomists who considered Asherah worship a fundamental threat to Yahwism. Their fears are adequately reflected in the harsh language of the deuteronomistic redactor(s) of Kings.

These same texts provide us with evidence that there were some rituals, sanctuaries, and even cultic utensils associated with the Asherah cult, as well as cultic personnel, at least prophets. They suggest that Asherah worship was widespread. It is interesting to note that the worship of Baal was also highly criticized, but the frequent purges seem to have met with success in eliminating or at least permanently reducing Baal worship by the Hebrews. This contrasts strongly with the effects of those same purges on Asherah worship. There was no lasting effect. Asherah worship always returned quickly. One suspects that the reason for this is that the cultic place of Baal, a male deity, was in direct and unresolvable conflict with the cultic place of Yahweh, while Asherah was not seen in popular piety as at all in conflict with Yahweh, but in perfect harmony. Thus there were Yahweh and Asherah, male and female deities, divine consorts. Both in Israel and in Judah Asherah remained a central cult figure. She was, as a maternal and fertility figure, attractive to the people. The Kings texts verify that she was worshiped nearly everywhere. There was even a cult of male prostitutes who in the name of Asherah would impregnate childless Hebrew women.

The Chronicler, although writing from a theological viewpoint different from the deuteronomistic historian of Kings, is in substantial agreement with the deuteronomist regarding Asherah worship. Many of the Chronicler's texts are taken from the texts of Kings. Thus the Chronicler sustains the deuteronomist's description of Asherah worship being present in both North and South throughout the monarchy. The Chronicler adds, however, that the goddess Asherah was identified not only with the wooden post, but with various other cultic objects, including incense altars and small figurines or images. She was identified with these in such a way that to abolish them would be to destroy her cult. No objects, no goddess.

The writers of both Kings and Chronicles refer to the growing confusion between Asherah and Astarte. Over the centuries the distinction between the two diminished. Their attributes became less distinguishable and their names were interchanged. The modern reader must beware of this tendency, keeping in mind that it was Asherah who was originally the goddess to be reckoned with. Only later was Astarte's name brought into the picture.

The prophets speak surprisingly little about Asherah. If ever there might be an argument asserting that Asherah worship in the Hebrew Bible was merely a deuteronomistic exaggeration, this would be it. The paucity of the prophetic references to Asherah worship is truly surprising. From another viewpoint, however, one would expect that if Asherah worship were important only to the deuteronomist, the prophets would mention her not at all. The very fact that the name Asherah comes up four times in three of the prophets, even though this is a small number, stands as a relatively strong testimony that there was some kind of Asherah worship in the Judah community.

There is no evidence which suggests that the Asherah worship against which the prophets spoke was different from that of the deuteronomist. Their use of the components of the meta-formula, pillars, idols, and altars, suggests that at least the compilers of Isaiah, Jeremiah, and Micah were quite aware of the problem and were also familiar with the language of those, who, like themselves, spoke out against it. Because of these similarities, it can be concluded that these prophetic texts refer to Asherah in a way similar to the deuteronomistic redactors.

There is another possible explanation for the paucity of references to Asherah in the prophetic books. It may be that the prophets were little concerned about Asherah worship. This is, of course, hypothetical. But if this is true, there are reasons. First, perhaps they did not consider Asherah worship a threat to Yahwism. Second, even if they did, perhaps it was less a threat than the other socio-political problems which captured their concern. In either case it would seem that the prophets focused their attention on problems other than Asherah. Moreover, it is possible that the prophetic redactors, many of whom were not deuteronomistic, had no particular need to speak against Asherah worship, and therefore did not include the name Asherah in their redactions, even if it might have appeared in the original prophetic sayings.

It is rare that archaeological evidence forms the foundation of air-tight arguments. Actually, by itself it proves very little. The evidence is, however, interesting and suggestive, and serves to support the arguments made more strongly by other means.

If there was Asherah worship, one would expect there to be some archaeological evidence which supports it. The absence of such evidence would not necessarily disprove that there was such worship. The presence of such evidence does not prove the theory, but it does remove some of the doubt.

Engle's arguments that certain figurines are images of Asherah is attractive to anyone whose hope is to show the presence of Asherah worship. Yet there remains no direct evidence, like an inscription of Asherah's name at the base of such a figurine, to tie the figurines to Asherah. It seems a likely possibility, but it is not yet proven.

Other evidence leaves a little more room for encouragement. The possibility of a socket for a wooden post in Gezer's sanctuary, the regularity of lions and certain characteristics like a particular hair style associated with Asherah, and the tree of life lead one to suspect that Asherah's characteristic representations are now becoming known.

Particularly noteworthy is that most of the artifacts are from Canaanite sites, not Hebrew sites. The artifacts seem to verify the presence of Asherah worship in Canaanite areas between 2000 and 700 B.C.E., which is no surprise, but say little about Hebrew worship during the time of the monarchy, from 1000 to 600 B.C.E. However, even this observation is suspect. Just because the more easily identifiable artifacts show worship at Canaanite sanctuaries rather than Hebrew sites does not deny the possibility that the Hebrews worshiped Asherah, even with great frequency. Who is to say that the Hebrews did not frequent Canaanite sanctuaries? It is entirely possible that they did. Evidence from Genesis suggests that they did. Abram, for example, visited the Canaanite sacred places at Shechem and Bethel (Genesis 12:6-8). What's more, since the foreign objects in the Hebrew sanctuaries were several times systematically purged, that is, burned and ground to powder, one would expect few if any of them to have survived.

Inscriptions are much more helpful to the argument that Asherah was worshiped by the Hebrews during the pre-exilic era. Especially helpful are the Kuntillet Ajrud and the Khirbet el-Qom inscriptions. They date from 800 to 700 B.C.E. and are Hebrew. They both associate Yahweh and Asherah in a cultic capacity, and affirm that the goddess Asherah was indeed held in high esteem by some of the Hebrews of that period.

A last question lingers. Was Asherah a goddess of the Israelites? One might answer, "No." She was heartily condemned by the deuteronomistic histories. Every passage of the Hebrew Bible which refers to her or to her cult object is an explicit condemnation of Asherah worship. The biblical authors were unanimous in their abhorrence of Asherah worship, which they considered an aberration of the highest order and a serious threat to the Yahwism they espoused.

One might also answer "Yes" to the question. While the biblical authors, especially the deuteronomistic school, were strongly opposed to Asherah worship, these authors did not themselves constitute the whole of ancient Israel. On the contrary, the abuses they condemned imply, by the fact that they were widespread and irrepressible, that the biblical authors were actually a rather small minority. The majority of the people, from state officials to peasants, worshiped Asherah. This is substantiated by the biblical texts, which show that, in spite of attempts by several of the kings of Israel and Judah to purge Asherah worship from the land, the people held steadfast to their devotion to Asherah. This devotion included an official cult with sanctuaries, cult personnel, and offerings. Moreover, the Asherah cult operated in, among other places, the Jerusalem Temple, where the image of Asherah stood for many years beside the altar of Yahweh, and where sexual rituals were performed in the name of Asherah. The people considered

Asherah the divine consort of Yahweh, just as in the Canaanite pantheon she had been the consort of El, the chief Canaanite god. Asherah was, without a doubt, popularly accepted as the goddess of Israel.

One might speculate further that the image of the divine Wisdom, which is depicted as female in the wisdom books, is in some way related, if not directly to the goddess Asherah, at least to a basic need within the Hebrew community to find the female dimension of the divine. Mark Smith describes the female Wisdom as an extension of the goddess Asherah in the religion of Israel.[2] The God of Israel was depicted as predominantly male. To their worship of Yahweh, then, the Israelites added the worship of a female deity, Asherah. Moreover, in this modern age, many in the Judeo-Christian tradition, those who have been taught about God with predominantly male images, are now pursuing female images of God. Some even worship Mary, whose role as mother is similar in a few ways to that of Asherah. It seems that humanity, in its most primal elements of religiosity, demands a deity who affirms the wholeness of humanity, that is, both male and female. One learns from Asherah and the Israelites that any religion which overemphasizes either the maleness of femaleness of its deity should expect to be "corrected" by popular practice to the contrary.

Notes

1 Saul M. Olyan, *Asherah and the Cult of Yahweh in Israel*, SBL Monograph Series, No. 34, (Atlanta, Georgia: Scholars Press, 1988): 34.

2 Mark Smith, "God Male and Female in the Old Testament: Yahweh and His 'Asherah,' " *Theological Studies* 48 (1987): 333-340.

Selected Bibliography

A. Books

Aharoni, Yohanan. *The Archeology of the Land of Israel from the Prehistoric Beginnings to the End of the First Temple Period.* Ed. Miriam Aharoni. Trans. Anson F. Rainey. Philadelphia: Westminster Press, 1982.

________. *Investigation at Lachish: The Sanctuary and the Residency (Lachish V).* Tel Aviv: Gateway Publishers, 1975.

________. *The Land of the Bible: A Historical Geography.* Rev. and enlarged ed. Trans. and ed. Anson F. Rainey. Philadelphia: Westminster Press, 1979.

Ahlström, G. W. *Aspects of Syncretism in Israelite Religion.* Lund: C. W. K. Gleerup, 1963.

Albright, William Foxwell. *Archaeology and the Religion of Israel.* Baltimore: Johns Hopkins Press, 1942.

________. *The Biblical Period from Abraham to Ezra.* New York: Harper Torchbook, 1963.

________. *From Stone Age to Christianity.* 2nd ed. New York: Doubleday Anchor Book, 1957.

________. *Yahweh and the Gods of Canaan: A Historical Analysis of Two Contrasting Faiths.* London: Athlone Press, 1968.

Allegro, John M. *The Chosen People: A Study of Jewish History from the Time of the Exile until the Revolt of Bar Kochba*. London and Toronto: Hodder and Stoughton Ltd., 1971.

Anati, Emmanuel. *Palestine Before the Hebrews: A History, from the Earliest Arrival of Man to the Conquest of Canaan*. New York: Alfred A. Knopf, 1963.

Anderson, G. W., ed. *Tradition & Interpretation: Essays by Members of the Society for Old Testament Study*. Oxford: Clarendon Press, 1979.

Barrois, A. G. *Manuel D'Archeologie Biblique*. Paris: A. and J. Picard, 1953.

Ben-Sasson, H. H., ed. *A History of the Jewish People*. Cambridge, Mass.: Harvard University Press, 1976.

Beyerlin, Walter, ed. *Near Eastern Religious Texts Relating to the Old Testament*. Philadelphia: Westminster Press, 1978.

Boling, Robert. *Judges*. Anchor Bible, vol. 6a. New York: Doubleday & Co., 1975.

Bright, John. *A History of Israel*. 3rd ed. Philadelphia: Westminster Press, 1981.

Bronner, Leah. *The Stories of Elijah and Elisha as Polemics Against Baal Worship*. Leiden: E. J. Brill, 1968.

Brown, Reymond E., et al, eds. *The Jerome Biblical Commentary*. Englewood Cliffs, New Jersey: Prentice-Hall, Inc., 1968.

Butterworth, E. A. S. *The Tree at the Navel of the Earth*. Berlin: Walter de Gruyter, 1970.

Cassuto, U. *The Goddess Anath.* Trans. Israel Abrahams. Jerusalem: The Magnes Press, The Hebrew University, 1971.

Childs, Brevard S. *The Book of Exodus: A Critical, Theological Commentary.* Philadelphia: Westminster Press, 1974.

Cornfeld, Gaalyah, and Freedman, David Noel. *Archaeology of the Bible, Book by Book.* San Francisco: Harper & Row, 1976.

Cross, Frank Moore. *Canaanite Myth and Hebrew Epic.* Cambridge: Harvard University Press, 1973.

de Moor, J. C. "Asherah." In *Theological Dictionary of the Old Testament.* Vol. 1, pp. 438-444. Edited by G. Johannes Botterweck and Helmer Ringgren. Grand Rapids: William B. Eerdmans, 1979.

de Vaux, Roland. *Ancient Israel.* 2 vols. New York: McGraw-Hill, 1965.

________. *The Bible and the Ancient Near East.* Trans. Damian McHugh. New York: Doubleday, 1971.

________. *The Early History of Israel.* Trans. David Smith. Philadelphia: Westminster Press, 1978.

de Vries, Simon J. *1 Kings.* World Biblical Commentary. Vol. 12. Waco, Texas: World Books, 1985.

Dietrich, Walter. *Israel und Kanaan: vom Ringen zweier Gesellschaftssysteme.* Stuttgarter Bibel-Studien, no. 94. Stuttgart: Verlag Katholisches Bibelwerk, 1979.

Driver, G. R. *Canaanite Myths and Legends.* Old Testament Studies, no. 3. Edinburgh: T. & T. Clark, 1956.

Eissfeldt, Otto. *The Old Testament: An Introduction*. Trans. P. Ackroyd. New York: Harper & Row, 1965.

Engle, James Robert. *Pillar Figurines of Iron Age Israel and Asherah/Asherim*. A dissertation for the University of Pittsburgh. Ann Arbor: University Microfilms International, 1980.

Finegan, Jack. *Archaeological History of the Ancient Middle East*. Boulder, Colorado: Westview Press, 1979.

________. *Light from the Ancient Past: The Archaeological Background of Judaism and Christianity*. 2nd ed. New Jersey: Princeton University Press, 1959.

Fisher, Loren, ed. *Ras Shamra Parallels: The Texts from Ugarit and the Hebrew Bible*. Vols. 1 and 2. Analecta Orientalia, nos. 49 and 50. Rome: Pontifical Biblical Institute, 1972 and 1975.

Gibson, J. C. L. *Canaanite Myths and Legends*. 2nd ed. Edinburgh: T. & T. Clark, 1978.

Gordon, Cyrus H. *Before the Bible: The Common Background of Greek and Hebrew Civilisations*. London: Collins, 1962.

________. *Ugarit and Minoan Crete: The Bearing of Their Texts on the Origins of Western Culture*. New York: W. W. Norton, 1966.

________. *Ugaritic Manual*. Analecta Orientalia, no. 35. Rome: Pontifical Biblical Institute, 1955.

________. *Ugaritic Textbook*. Analecta Orientalia, no. 38. Rome: Pontificial Biblical Institute, 1965.

Gottwald, Norman K. *The Tribes of Yahweh*. Maryknoll, New York: Orbis Books, 1979.

Goulder, Michael D. *The Psalms of the Sons of Korah.* Journal for the Study of the Old Testament Supplement Series, no. 20. Sheffield, England: JSOT Press, 1982.

Gray, John. *I & II Kings: A Commentary.* 2nd ed. Philadelphia: Westminster, 1970.

________. *The Canaanites.* Ancient Peoples and Places, no. 38. London: Thames and Hudson, 1964.

________. *The KRT Text in the Literature of Ras Shamra.* 2nd ed. Leiden: E. J. Brill, 1964.

________. *The Legacy of Canaan: The Ras Shamra Texts and Their Relevance to the Old Testament.* Supplements to Vetus Testamentum, no. 5. Leiden: E. J. Brill, 1957.

________. *Near Eastern Mythology.* New York: Hamlyn Publishing Group, 1969.

Habel, Norman C. *Yahweh Versus Baal: A Conflict of Religious Cultures.* New York: Bookman Associates, 1964.

Haran, Menahem. *Temples and Temple-Service in Ancient Israel: An Inquiry into the Character of Cult Phenomena and the Historical Setting of the Priestly School.* Oxford: The Clarendon Press, 1978.

Harrelson, Walter. *From Fertility Cult to Worship.* New York: Doubleday, Anchor Book, 1970.

Harris, Zellig S. *Development of the Canaanite Dialects: An Investigation in Linguistic History.* American Oriental Series, no. 16. New Haven, Conn.: American Oriental Society, 1939; reprinted ed., Millwood, New York: Kraus Reprint, 1978.

Hertzberg, Hans Wilhelm. *I & II Samuel: A Commentary*. Trans. J. S. Bowden. Philadelphia: Westminster Press, 1960.

Hillers, Delbert R. *Micah*. Paul D. Hanson and Loren Fisher, eds. Philadelphia: Fortress Press, 1984.

Hommages a Andre DuPont-Sommer. Paris: Libraire d'Amerique et d'Orient, Adrien-Maisonneuve, 1971.

Hölscher, G. "Das Buch der Könige, seine Quellen und seine Redaktion." In *Eucharisterion Hermann Gunkel zum 60. Geburtstag*. Forschungen zur Religion und Literatur des Alten und Neuen Testaments. Vol. 36. Göttingen: Vandenhoeck & Ruprecht, 1927.

Jacob, Edmond. *Ras Shamra-Ugarit et L'Ancien Testament*. Paris: Delachaux et Niestle, 1960.

Jastrow, Marcus. *Dictionary of the Targum: The Talmud Babli and Yerushalmi, and the Midrashic Literature*. New York: Pardes Publishing House, 1950.

Jepsen, A. *Die Quellen des Königsbuches*. 2nd ed. Halle: M. Niemeyer, 1956.

Jirku, Anton. *Die Ausgrabungen in Palästina und Syrien*. 2nd ed. Graz, Austria: Akademische Druck und Verlagsanstalt, 1970.

Kaiser, Otto. *Isaiah 13-39: A Commentary*. Philadelphia: Westminster Press, 1974.

Kapelrud, Arvid S. *Baal in the Ras Shamra Texts*. Copenhagen: G. E. C. Gad, 1952.

________. *The Ras Shamra Discoveries and the Old Testament*. Trans. G. W. Anderson. Tulsa Oklahoma: University of Oklahoma Press, 1963.

Kaufmann, Yehezkel. *The Religion of Israel from Its Beginnings to the Babylonian Exile*. Trans. and abridged by Moshe Greenberg. New York: Schoken Books, 1972.

Kenyon, Frederic. *The Bible and Archaeology*. New York: Harper, 1949.

Kenyon, Kathleen M. *Amorites and Canaanites*. London: Oxford University Press, 1966.

________. *Archaeology in the Holy Land*. 3rd ed. London: Ernest Benn, 1970.

________. *The Bible and Recent Archaeology*. Atlanta: John Knox, 1978.

Kuenen, A. *The Religion of Israel to the Fall of the Jewish State*. Trans. Alfred H. May. London: Williams and Norgate, 1882.

La Sor, William Sanford, et al. *Old Testament Survey: The Message, Form, and Background of the Old Testament*. Grand Rapids: William B. Eerdmans Publishing Co., 1982.

L'Heureux, Conrad E. *Rank Among the Canaanite Gods*. Missoula, Montana: Scholars Press, 1979.

Mansoor, Menahem, ed. *The Book and the Spade: A Guide to Biblical Archaeology*. 3rd ed. Madison: Office of the Exhibition the Book and the Spade, 1975.

Matthiae, Paolo. *Ebla: An Empire Rediscovered*. Trans. Christopher Holmes. New York: Doubleday, 1981.

Mays, James Luther. *Micah: A Commentary*. Philadelphia: Westminster Press, 1976.

McCurley, Foster R. *Ancient Myths and Biblical Faith: Scriptural Transformations*. Philadelphia: Fortress Press, 1983.

Mendelhall, George E. *The Tenth Generation: The Origins of the Biblical Tradition*. Baltimore: Johns Hopkins University Press, 1973.

Mullen, E. Theodore, Jr. *The Divine Council in Canaanite and Early Hebrew Literature*. Harvard Semitic Monographs, no. 24. Chico, California: Scholars Press, 1980.

Myers, Jacob M. *I Chronicles*. Anchor Bible, vol. 12. New York: Doubleday & Co., 1965.

________. *II Chronicles*. Anchor Bible, vol. 13. New York: Doubleday & Co., 1965.

Negbi, Ora. *Canaanite Gods in Metal: An Archaeological Study of Ancient Syro-Palestinian Figurines*. Tel Aviv: Tel Aviv University Institute of Archaeology, 1976.

Nicholson, Ernest W. *Deuteronomy and Tradition*. Philadelphia: Fortress Press, 1967.

Noth, Martin. *The History of Israel*. 2nd ed. New York: Harper & Row, 1960.

Noth, Martin. *Überlieferungsgeschichtliche Studien I*. Tübingen: M. Niemeyer, 1957.

Oden, R. A., Jr. *Studies in Lucian's "De Syria Dea"*. Harvard Semitic Museum, no. 15. Missoula, Montana: Scholars Press, Press, 1977.

Oldenburg, Ulf. *The Conflict Between El and Baal in Canaanite Religion*. Leiden: E. J. Brill, 1969.

Orlinsky, Harry M. *Understanding the Bible Through History and Archaeology*. New York: KTAV, 1972.

Parrot, Andre. "Autels et installations cultuelles a Mari." In *Congress Volume: Copenhagen 1953*, pp. 112-119. Ed. G. W. Anderson, et al. Supplements to Vetus Testamentum, no. 1. Leiden: E. J. Brill, 1953.

Patai, Raphael. *The Hebrew Goddess*. New York: Avon, Discus Book, 1978.

Perlman, Alice Lenore. *Asherah and Astarte in the Old Testament and Ugaritic Literature*. A dissertation for the Graduate Theological Union, Berkeley. Ann Arbor: University Microfilms International, 1979.

Pettinato, Giovanni. *The Archives of Ebla: An Empire Inscribed in Clay*. New York: Doubleday, 1981.

Polzin, Robert. *Moses and the Deuteronomist: A Literary Study of the Deuteronomic History, Part One*. New York: Seabury Press, 1980.

Pope, Marvin H. *El in the Ugaritic Texts*. Supplements to Vetus Testamentum, no. 2. Leiden: E. J. Brill, 1955.

Porten, Bezalel. *Archives from Elephantine: The Life of an Ancient Jewish Military Colony*. Berkeley: University of California Press, 1968.

Pritchard, James B. *Archaeology and the Old Testament*. New Jersey: Princeton University Press, 1958.

________. *Palestinian Figurines in Relation to Certain Goddesses Known Through Literature*. New Haven: American Oriental Society, 1943.

Pritchard, James B., ed. *The Ancient Near East: An Anthology of Texts and Pictures*. Vol. 1. New Jersey: Princeton University Press, 1958.

_______. *Ancient Near Eastern Texts Relating to the Old Testament*. 3rd ed. with supp. New Jersey: Princeton University Press, 1969.

_______. *The Ancient Near East in Pictures Relating to the Old Testament*. 2nd ed. with supp. New Jersey: Princeton University Press, 1969.

Rad, Gerhard von. *Deuteronomy: A Commentary*. Trans. Dorothea Barton. Philadelphia: Westminster Press, 1966.

Reed, William L. *The Asherah in the Old Testament*. Fort Worth: Texas Christian University, 1949.

Ringgren, Helmer. *Israelite Religion*. Trans. David E. Green. Philadelphia: Fortress Press, 1975.

_______. "Israel's Place Among the Religions of the Ancient Near East." In *Studies in the Religion of Ancient Israel*, pp. 1-8. Ed. G. W. Anderson, et al. Supplements to Vetus Testamentum, no. 23. Leiden: E. J. Brill, 1972.

_______. *Religions of the Ancient Near East*. Trans. John Sturdy. Philadelphia: Westminster Press, 1973.

Robinson, J. *The First Book of Kings*. Cambridge Bible Commentary. Vol. 25. Cambridge: Cambridge University Press, 1972.

Rummel, Stan, ed. *Ras Shamra Parallels*. Vol. 3. Analecta Orientalia, no. 51. Rome: Pontifical Biblical Institute, 1981.

Schauss, Hayyim. *The Jewish Festivals: History and Observance.* Trans. Samuel Jaffe. New York: Schocken Books, 1962.

________. *The Lifetime of a Jew Throughout the Ages of Jewish History.* New York: Union of American Hebrew Congregations, 1950.

Schmidt, Werner H. *Königtum Gottes in Ugarit und Israel.* Beihefte zur Zeitschrift für die Alttestamentliche Wissenschaft. Berlin: Verlag Alfed Töpelmann, 1966.

________. *Old Testament Introduction.* Trans. Matthew J. O'Connell. New York: Crossroad, 1984.

Sellin, Ernst and Fohrer, Georg. *Introduction to the Old Testament.* Trans. David E. Green. Nashville: Abingdon, 1968.

Shanks, Hershel, ed. *Recent Archaeology in the Land of Israel.* Trans. Aryeh Finklestein. Washington, D.C.: Biblical Archaeology Society, 1984.

Smith, Morton. *Palestinian Parties and Politics That Shaped the Old Testament.* New York: Columbia University Press, 1971.

Soggin, J. Alberto. *Judges: A Commentary.* Philadelphia: Westminster Press, 1981.

Spuler, B., ed. *Handbuch der Orientalistik.* Vol. 1. Leiden: E. J. Brill, 1964.

Teixidor, Javier. *The Pagan God: Popular Religion in the Greco-Roman Near East.* Princeton, New Jersey: Princeton University Press, 1977.

Thomas, D. Winton, ed. *Archaeology and Old Testament Study.* Oxford: Clarendon Press, 1967.

_______. *Documents from Old Testament Times.* New York: Harper, Torchbook, 1958.

Vaughan, Patrick H. *The Meaning of "BAMA" in the Old Testament.* Cambridge, England: Cambridge University Press, 1974.

Watters, William R. *Formula Criticism and the Poetry of the Old Testament.* New York: Walter de Gruyter, 1976.

Weingreen, J. *Introduction to the Critical Study of the Text of the Hebrew Bible.* New York: Oxford University Press, 1982.

Whitaker, Richard E. *A Concordance of the Ugaritic Literature.* Massachusetts: Harvard University Press, 1972.

Williamson, H. G. M. *1 and 2 Chronicles.* New Century Bible Commentary. Grand Rapids: William B. Eerdmans, 1982.

Wiseman, D. J., ed. *Peoples of Old Testament Times.* Oxford: Claredon Press, 1973.

Wright, G. Ernest. *Biblical Archaeology.* 2nd ed. Philadelphia: Westminster Press, 1962.

_______. *The Old Testament Against Its Environment.* Naperville, IL: Alec R. Allenson, 1950.

Würthwein, Ernst. *The Text of the Old Testament: An Introduction to the Biblia Hebraeica.* Trans. Erroll F. Rhodes. Grand Rapids: William B. Eerdmans, 1979.

Yamashita, Tadanori. *The Goddess Asherah.* A dissertation for Yale University. Ann Arbor: University Microfilms International, 1964.

Young, Gordon D., ed. *Ugarit in Retrospect: 50 Years of Ugarit and Ugaritic*. Winona Lake, Indiana: Eisenbrauns, 1981.

B. Periodicals

Albright, William Foxwell. "A Prince of Taanach in the Fifteenth Century B.C." *Bulletin of the American Schools of Oriental Research* 94 (1944): 12-27.

________. "A Vow to Asherah in the Keret Epic." *Bulletin of the American Schools of Oriental Research* 94 (1944): 30-31.

Althann, Robert. "Ugarit, Ebla, and the Old Testament." *Bible Today* 97 (1978): 1710-1715.

Angerstorfer, Andreas. "Asherah als 'Consort of Jahwe' oder Asirtah?" *Biblische Notizen* 17 (1982): 7-16.

Avigad, Nahaman. "A Hebrew Seal Depicting a Sailing Ship." *Bulletin of the American Schools of Oriental Research* 246 (1982): 59-62.

Beck, Parhiya. "The Drawings from Horvat Teiman (Kuntillet Ajrud)." *Tel Aviv* 9 (1982): 29-31.

Ben-Aire, Sara. "A Mould for a Goddess Plaque." *Israel Exploration Journal* 33 (1983): 72-77.

________. "A Pottery Mould for a Goddess Figurine." *Qadmoniot* 16 (1983): 123-124. (Hebrew).

Bernhardt, Karl-Heinz. "Asherah in Ugarit und im Alten Testament." *Mitteilungen des Instituts für Orientforschung der Deutschen Akademie der Wissenschaften zu Berlin* 13 (1967): 163-174.

Betlyon, John Wilson. "The Cult of Asherah/Elat at Sidon." *Journal of Near Eastern Studies* 44 (1985): 53-56.

Biale, David. "The God with Breasts: El Shaddai in the Bible." *History of Religions* 20 (1982): 240-256.

Bordreuil, Pierre. "Michee 4:10-13 et ses Paralleles Ougaritiques." *Semitica* 21 (1971): 21-28.

Boraas, Roger S. "Of Serpents and Gods." *Dialog* 17 (1978): 273-279.

Chase, D. A. "A Note on an Inscription from Kuntillet Ajrud." *Bulletin of the Association of American Schools of Oriental Research* 246 (1982): 63-7.

Clamer, Christa. "A Gold Plaque from Tel Lachish." *Tel Aviv* 7 (1980): 152-162.

Cohen, Rudolph. "The Fortresses King Solomon Built to Protect His Southern Border." *Biblical Archaeology Review* 11 (1985): 56-70.

Cross, Frank Moore, Jr. "The Evolution of the Proto-Canaanite Alphabet." *Bulletin of the American Schools of Oriental Research* 134 (1954): 15-24.

_______. "The Origin and Early Evolution of the Alphabet." *Eretz Israel* 8 (1967): 8-24.

_______. "A Reconstruction of the Judean Restoration." *Journal of Biblical Literature* 94 (1975): 4-18.

Cross, Frank Moore, Jr. and Saley, Richard J. "Phoenician Incantation on a Plaque of the Seventh Century B.C. from Arslan Tash in Upper Syria." *Bulletin of the American Schools of Oriental Research* 197 (1970): 42-49.

Day, John. "Asherah in the Hebrew Bible and Northwest Semitic Literature. *Journal of Biblical Literature* 105 (1986): 385-408.

Dever, William G. "Asherah, Consort of Yahweh? New Evidence from Kuntillet Ajrud." *Bulletin of the American Schools of Oriental Research* 255 (1984): 21-37.

_______. "Iron Age Epigraphic Material from Khirbet El-Kom." *Hebrew Union College Annual* 50-51 (1969-70): 139-204.

_______. "Recent Archaeological Confirmation of the Cult of Asherah in Ancient Israel." *Hebrew Studies* 23 (1982): 37-43.

Dohmen, Von Christoph. "Heisst Semel 'Bild Statue'?" *Zeitschrift für die alttestamentliche Wissenschaft* 96 (1984): 263-66.

Dothan, M. "The Excavations at Nahariyah." *Israel Exploration Journal* 6 (1956): 14-25.

Dunand, Maurice. "Le Temple de'Echmoun a Sidon: Essai de chronologie." *Bulletin du Musee de Beyrouth* 26 (1973): 10-12.

Emerton, John A. "New Light on Israelite Religion: The Implications of the Inscriptions from Kuntillet Ajrud." *Zeitschrift für die alttestamentliche Wissenschaft* 94 (1982): 2-20.

_______. "The 'Second Bull' in Judges 6:25-28." *Erets Yisrael* 14 (1978): 52-55.

Freedman, David Noel. "Yahweh of Samaria and his Asherah." *Biblical Archaeologist* (December, 1987): 241-249.

Gilula, Mordecai. "To Yahweh Shomron and His Asherah." (Hebrew) *Shenaton* 3 (1978-79): 128-37.

Giveon, Raphael. "Remarks on the Tel Qarnayim Goddess." *Biblische Notizen* 33 (1986): 7-9.

Grintz, J. M. "Some Observations on the 'High Place' in the History of Israel." *Vetus Testamentum* 27 (1977): 111-113.

Hestrin, Ruth. "The Lachish Ewer and the Asherah." *Israel Exploration Journal* 37 (1987): 212-223.

Höffken, Peter. "Eine Bemerkung zum religionsgeschichtlichen Hintergrund von Dtn 6,4." *Biblische Zeitschrift* 28 (1984): 88-93.

Ishida, Tomoo. "The Structure and Historical Implications of the Lists of Pre-Israelite Nations." *Biblica* 50 (1979): 461-490.

Jaros, Karl. "Zur Inschrift Nr. 3 von Hirbet el-Qom." *Biblische Notizen* 19 (1982): 31-40.

Joines, Karen Randolph. "The Bronze Serpent in the Israelite Cult." *Journal of Biblical Literature* 87 (1968): 245-56.

Kinet, Dirk. "Ugarit, Fünfzig Jahre Forschung in einer Stadt aus der Umwelt des Alten Testaments." *Bibel und Kirche* 4 (1981): 285-88.

King, Philip J. "The Contribution of Archaeology to Biblical Studies." *Catholic Biblical Quarterly* 45 (1983): 1-16.

Kjeseth, Peter. "Nehushtan and Ernst Bloch--Raymond Brown and Biblical Studies." *Dialog* 17 (1978): 280-86.

Korr, Craig S. "Evidence of the Sign of the Goddess Tanit in the Theban Region of Egypt." *Israel Exploration Journal* 31 (1981): 94-95.

Lamp, Herbert F. "An Old Testament Index to Archaeological Sources." *Trinity Journal* 3NS (1982): 170-194.

Lapp, Paul W. "The 1968 Excavations at Tell Ta'annek." *Bulletin of the American Schools of Oriental Research* 195 (1969): 2-49.

Lehmann, M. R. "A New Interpretation of the Term *sdmwt.*" *Vetus Testamentum* 3 (1953): 361-71.

Le Maire, Andre. "Les Inscriptions de Khirbet El-Qom et L'Asherah de YHWH." *Revue Biblique* 4 (1977): 595-608.

________. "Who or What Was Yahweh's Asherah?" *Biblical Archaeology Review* 10 (1984): 42-51.

Lipinski, Edward. "The Goddess Atirat in Ancient Arabia, in Babylon, and in Ugarit." *Orientalis Lovaniensia Periodica* 3 (1972): 101-119.

MacLaurin, E. C. B. "The Canaanite Background of the Doctrine of the Virgin Mary." *Religious Traditions* 3 (1980): 1-11.

Meshel, Ze'ev. "Did Yahweh Have a Consort? The New Religious Inscriptions from the Sinai." *Biblical Archaeology Review* 5 (1979): 24-35.

________. "Kuntillet Ajrud: An Israelite Religious Center in Northern Sinai." *Expedition* 20 (1978): 50-54.

Michel, Walter L. "BTWLH, 'Virgin' or 'Virgin (Anat)' in Job 31:1?" *Hebrew Studies* 23 (1982): 59-66.

Miller, J. Maxwell. "Archaeology and Israelite Conquest of Canaan: Some Methodological Observations." *Palestine Exploration Quarterly* 109 (1977): 87-93.

Miller, Patrick D., Jr. "Ugarit and the History of Religions." *Journal of Northwest Semitic Languages* 9 (1981): 119-128.

Mittmann, Siegfried. "Die Grabenschrift des Sängers Uriahu." *Zeitschrift Verein des deutsche Palästina-Vereins* 97 (1981): 139-152.

Murmelstein, B. "Spuren altorientalischer Einflüsse im rabbinischen Schriftum." *Zeitschrift für die alttestamentliche Wissenschaft* 81 (1969): 223-5.

Mutius, Hans-Georg von. "Die Bibelzitate im Seder Elijahu Rabba." *Biblische Notizen* 9 (1979): 28-30.

Naveh, Joseph. "Graffiti and Dedications." *Bulletin of the American Schools of Oriental Research* 235 (1979): 27-30.

Ogden, Graham S. "The Northern Extent of Josiah's Reforms." *Australian Biblical Review* 26 (1978): 26-34.

Oden, R. A., Jr. "Ba'al Samem and El." *Catholic Biblical Quarterly* 39 (1977): 457-73.

________. "The Persistence of Canaanite Religion." *Biblical Archaeologist* 39 (1976): 31-36.

Paltiel, E. "Ethnicity and the State in the Kingdom of Ugarit." *Abr Nahrain* 19 (1980-81): 43-61.

Patai, Raphael. "The Goddess Asherah." *Journal of Near Eastern Study* 24 (1965): 37-52.

Rendtorff, Rolf. "El, Ba'al, und Jahwe." *Zeitschrift für die alttestamentliche Wissenschaft* 78 (1966): 277-292.

Rosenbaum, Jonathan. "Hezekiah's Reform and Deuteronomistic Tradition." *Harvard Theological Review* 72 (1979): 23-43.

Schaeffer, C. F. A. "Le fouilles de Minet-el-Beida et de Ras Shamra." *Syria* 13 (1932): 1-27.

Schaeffer, C. F. A. "Noveaux temoinages de culte de El et de Baal a Ras Shamra-Ugarit et ailleurs en Syrie-Palestine." *Syria* 43 (1966): 1-19.

Smith, Mark. "God Male and Female in the Old Testament: Yahweh and his 'Asherah.' " *Theological Studies* 48 (1987): 333-340.

Taylor, J. Glen. "The Song of Deborah and Two Canaanite Goddesses." *Journal for the Study of the Old Testament* 23 (1982): 99-108.

Ussishkin, David. "The 'Lachish Reliefs' and the City of Lachish." *Israel Exploration Journal* 30 (1980): 174-195.

Worden, T. "The Literary Influence of the Ugaritic Fertility Myth on the Old Testament." *Vetus Testamentum* 3 (1953): 273-299.